Congressional Research Service

Informing the legislative debate since 1914 _____

Turkey: Background and U.S. Relations

Jim Zanotti
Specialist in Middle Eastern Affairs

August 1, 2014

Congressional Research Service

7-5700

www.crs.gov

R41368

Summary

Several Turkish domestic and foreign policy issues have significant relevance for U.S. interests, and Congress plays an active role in shaping and overseeing U.S. relations with Turkey. This report provides background information on Turkey and discusses possible policy options for Members of Congress and the Obama Administration. U.S. relations with Turkey—a longtime North Atlantic Treaty Organization (NATO) ally—have evolved over time. Turkey's economic dynamism and geopolitical importance have increased its influence regionally and globally. Although Turkey still depends on the United States and other NATO allies for political and strategic support, its increased economic and military self-reliance since the Cold War allows Turkey relatively greater opportunity for an assertive role in foreign policy. Greater Turkish independence of action and continuing political transformation appear to have been mutually reinforcing—with both led for more than a decade by Prime Minister Recep Tayyip Erdogan and the Islamist-rooted Justice and Development Party (AKP). However, it remains unclear how Turkey might reconcile majoritarian views favoring Turkish nationalism and Sunni Muslim values with secular governance and protection of individual freedoms and minority rights, including with regard to Turkey's Kurdish citizens.

The record of U.S.-Turkey cooperation during the Obama Administration has been mixed. To some extent it mirrors the complexities that past U.S. administrations faced with Turkey in reconciling bilateral alignment on general foreign policy objectives with substantive points of disagreement involving countries such as Greece, Cyprus, Armenia, and Iraq. Patterns in the U.S.-Turkey bilateral relationship indicate that both countries seek to minimize damage resulting from disagreements. However, these patterns also suggest that periodic fluctuations in how the two countries' interests converge may persist. It is unclear how this dynamic might affect the extent to which future U.S. approaches to regional issues involve Turkey, or might affect the countries' efforts to increase closeness in other facets of their political and economic relationship.

Congress has shown considerable interest in the following issues:

- U.S.-Turkey cooperation and consultation in the Middle East regarding major regional security issues involving Syria, Iraq, Iran, and Afghanistan;

- Difficulties in Turkey's relations with Israel, prospects of their improvement, and how those might affect U.S.-Turkey relations;

- A possible deal between Turkey and a Chinese government-owned company to co-produce a Turkish air and missile defense system, which could have implications for U.S.-Turkey defense cooperation and for Turkey's political and military profile within NATO;

- A potential congressional resolution or presidential statement that could recognize World War I-era actions by the Ottoman Empire (Turkey's predecessor state) against hundreds of thousands of Armenians as genocide; and

- Domestic developments in Turkey in light of major protests in June 2013, apparent power struggles among key actors following subsequent corruption-related allegations, and upcoming elections in 2014 and 2015.

Many U.S. policymakers also are interested in the rights of minority Christian communities within Turkey; the currently stalemated prospects of Turkish accession to the European Union (EU); promoting increased trade with Turkey; and Turkey's role in the Cyprus dispute.

Contents

Figures

Tables

Appendixes

Contacts

Introduction and Issues for Congress

As global challenges to U.S. interests have changed over time, U.S. relations with Turkey—an important North Atlantic Treaty Organization (NATO) ally since the Cold War era—have evolved. Congress plays an active role in shaping and overseeing U.S. relations with Turkey. Several Turkish domestic and foreign policy issues have significant relevance for U.S. interests.

Gauging how U.S. and Turkish interests coincide has become increasingly complicated. Political transition and unrest in the Middle East since 2011 appear to have contributed to the following dynamic between the two countries:

- Turkish leaders seem to perceive a need for U.S. help to defend its borders and backstop regional stability, given threats and potential threats from various states and non-state actors; and

- The United States may be more dependent on its alliance with Turkey to forward U.S. interests in the region following the end of the U.S. military mission in Iraq and other possible future reductions in its Middle East footprint.

These factors have led to frequent high-level U.S.-Turkey consultation on developments in Syria, Iraq, and the broader region. The two countries may agree on a general vision of using political and economic linkages—backed by some level of security—to achieve and improve regional stability and encourage free markets and democratic mechanisms. However, it appears that they periodically differ regarding how to achieve this vision, such as when questions arise about which third-party actors—Israel, the Asad regime, Iraq's government, Kurdish groups, Al Qaeda affiliates, Palestinian factions, Iran, Russia, and China—should be tolerated, involved, bolstered, or opposed. Priorities and threat perceptions may differ in part due to the United States's geographical remoteness from the region, contrasted with Turkey's proximity.

Turkey in Brief	
Population:	75,627,384 (2012 est.)
Area:	783,562 sq km (302,535 sq. mi., slightly larger than Texas)
Most Populous Cities:	Istanbul 13.85 mil., Ankara 4.97 mil., Izmir 4.01 mil., Bursa 2.69 mil., Adana 2.13 mil. (2012 est.)
Ethnic Groups:	Turks 70%-75%; Kurds 18%; Other minorities 7%-12% (2008 est.)
Religion:	Muslim 99.8% (Sunni 75%-88%, Alevi 12%-25%), Others (mainly Christian and Jewish) 0.2%
Literacy:	87% (male 95%, female 80%) (2004 est.)
% of Population 14 or Younger:	24.9% (2012 est.)
GDP Per Capita:	$10,504 ($15,066 at purchasing power parity) (2012 est.)
Real GDP Growth:	3.9% (2013 est.)
Inflation:	7.6% (2013 est.)
Unemployment:	9.3% (2013 est.)
Budget Deficit:	1.6% (2013 est.)
Public Debt as % of GDP:	36.0% (2013 est.)
External Debt as % of GDP:	44.4% (2013 est.)
Current Account Deficit as % of GDP:	7.4% (2013 est.)
Sources: Turkish Statistical Institute; Economist Intelligence Unit; Central Intelligence Agency, *The World Factbook.*	

Members of Congress have expressed considerable interest regarding Turkey with respect to the following issues and questions:

- *Addressing Regional Change in the Greater Middle East*: Will Turkey's policies and actions be reconcilable with U.S. interests in countries such as Syria, Iraq, Egypt, and Afghanistan with regard to various actors and desired outcomes, particularly if they directly implicate Turkish security concerns or involve Turkish territory, military bases, and/or personnel? To what extent is Turkey willing and able to curb the influence of actors such as Iran that have historically opposed U.S. regional influence?

- *Israel and the U.S.-Turkey Relationship*: What are prospects for future Turkey-Israel relations? How might these relations affect U.S. efforts at regional security coordination? If Turkey-Israel tensions persist, should they affect congressional views generally on Turkey's status as a U.S. ally?

- *Turkey's Relationships with China and Other Non-NATO Countries*: How do and should Turkey's non-NATO relationships, especially its apparent intention—announced in September 2013—to partner with a Chinese government-owned company in developing an air and missile defense system, affect its political and military profile within the alliance?

- *Armenian Genocide Resolution*: What are the arguments for and against a potential U.S. congressional resolution or presidential statement characterizing World War I-era deaths of hundreds of thousands of Armenians through actions of the Ottoman Empire (Turkey's predecessor state) authorities as genocide? How would such a resolution or statement affect U.S.-Turkey relations and defense cooperation?

- *Rights of Non-Muslim Minority Religions*: What is Congress's proper role in promoting the rights of established Christian and Jewish communities within Turkey?

Many U.S. policymakers also are interested in the largely stalemated prospects of Turkish accession to the European Union (EU); promoting increased trade with Turkey; and Turkey's role in the decades-long dispute between ethnic Greek and ethnic Turkish populations regarding control of Cyprus.

Domestic developments in Turkey gained greater international attention in June 2013 when protests of a construction project near Istanbul's main square grew into more than two weeks of generalized demonstrations criticizing the still largely popular rule of Prime Minister Recep Tayyip Erdogan and his Justice and Development Party (known by its Turkish acronym, AKP). The authorities' assertive actions to quell the demonstrations have been widely criticized, along with Erdogan's apparent acceptance and perhaps encouragement of political polarization in likely anticipation of crucial 2014 and 2015 elections.[1] Then, on December 17, 2013, corruption-related arrests of a number of individuals with links to Erdogan and other cabinet ministers triggered a

---

[1] For more information on the protests, the government's response, and continuing consequences, see the State Department's 2013 Country Report on Human Rights for Turkey; and Bipartisan Policy Center, *From Rhetoric to Reality: Reframing U.S.-Turkey Policy*, Ambassadors Morton I. Abramowitz and Eric S. Edelman, Co-Chairs, October 2013, pp. 7, 20.

number of developments that have had a number of implications for Turkey's political and economic trajectory (see "Recent Domestic Controversies" below).

As a consequence, U.S. and EU officials and observers have perhaps become more attuned to concerns regarding civil liberties and checks and balances in Turkey, partly because of their potential to affect Turkey's economic viability and regional political role. However, it is unclear to what extent non-Turkish actors will play a significant role in resolving unanswered questions regarding Turkey's commitment to democracy and limited government, its secular-religious balance, and its Kurdish question.

According to the Turkish Coalition of America, a non-governmental organization that promotes positive Turkish-American relations, as of August 1, 2014, there are at least 142 Members (136 of whom are voting Members) of Congress in the Congressional Caucus (including three Senators) on Turkey and Turkish Americans.[2]

---

[2] See http://www.tc-america.org/in-congress/caucus htm.

Figure 1. Turkey and Its Neighbors

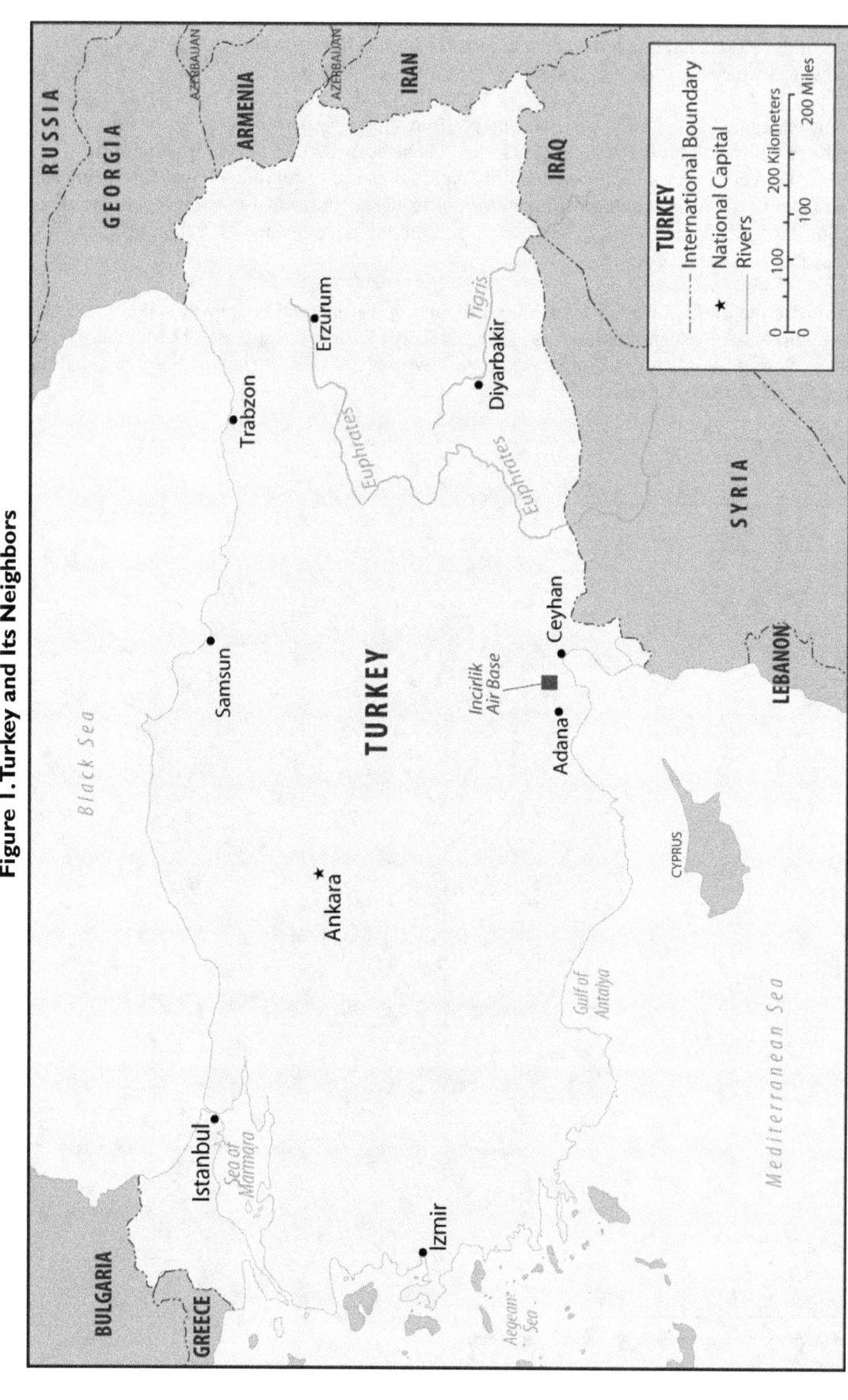

Source: CRS Graphics.

U.S.-Turkey Relations

Overview

The United States and Turkey have enjoyed a decades-long alliance. The calculations that led the United States to invest heavily in Turkey's defense and its military and economic development during the Cold War have evolved as the dynamics within both countries and the regional and global environments have changed. Another change has been Turkey's decreased dependence on U.S. material support and its increased assertiveness as a foreign policy actor, particularly in the Middle East and within international institutions such as the United Nations and the G-20, where it is scheduled to assume the yearly rotating presidency in 2015. One conceptualization of Turkey's importance to U.S. interests identifies it—along with India, Brazil, and Indonesia—as a "global swing state" with the ability to have a sizeable impact on international order, depending on how it engages with the United States and the rest of the world.[3]

At the outset of the Obama Administration, U.S. officials made clear their intent to emphasize the importance of a multifaceted strategic relationship with Turkey. In April 2009, President Obama, speaking of a "model partnership," visited Turkey during his first presidential trip abroad and addressed its Parliament in Ankara. He said that "Turkey is a critical ally.... And Turkey and the United States must stand together—and work together—to overcome the challenges of our time."

The record of U.S.-Turkey cooperation since then has been mixed. To some extent it mirrors the complexities that past U.S. administrations faced with Turkey in reconciling bilateral alignment on general foreign policy objectives with substantive points of disagreement involving countries such as Greece, Cyprus, Armenia, and Iraq.[4] For example, with regard to Iraq, Turkey cooperated with the United States in the 1991 Gulf War and following the U.S.-led 2003 Iraq invasion, but the Turkish parliamentary decision in 2003 not to allow U.S. forces to use its territory to open a northern front significantly affected U.S.-Turkey relations. The decision showed the United States that it could no longer rely primarily on past legacies of cooperation and close ties with the Turkish military.[5]

Given Turkey's increasing relevance as a Middle Eastern actor, U.S. officials seem to have viewed Turkey as well-positioned to be a facilitator of U.S. interests in the region as the United States has wound down its troop presence in Iraq, and is winding it down in Afghanistan. Turkish Prime Minister Recep Tayyip Erdogan and Foreign Minister Ahmet Davutoglu appear to have encouraged this approach by articulating a vision through which they have indicated that Turkey could help maintain regional stability while also promoting greater political and trade liberalization in neighboring countries. This vision—aspects of which Davutoglu has expressed at times through phrases such as "strategic depth" or "zero problems with neighbors"—draws upon Turkey's historical, cultural, and religious knowledge of and ties with other regional actors, as

---

[3] Daniel M. Kliman and Richard Fontaine, *Global Swing States: Brazil, India, Indonesia, Turkey, and the Future of International Order*, German Marshall Fund of the United States and Center for a New American Security, November 2012.

[4] For more background, see "Key Foreign Policy Issues" and **Appendix E**.

[5] For further information, see archived CRS Report R41761, *Turkey-U.S. Defense Cooperation: Prospects and Challenges*, by Jim Zanotti.

well as its soft power appeal as a Muslim-majority democracy with a robust and dynamic economy.[6]

Cooperation and Challenges in the Middle East and NATO

Turkey's regional political influence and expertise has been a key consideration in active U.S.-Turkey efforts to coordinate policy on a wide range of important and complicated issues, and is likely to continue to figure into U.S. regional calculations going forward. Nevertheless, some events during the Obama Administration appear to show that Turkey's ability to shape events may be less than imagined or suggested—as in the case of its unsuccessful efforts to mediate an end or reduction of civil conflict in both Libya and Syria.[7] Also, as Turkey has increased its links to the region, its heightened sensitivity to Middle Eastern public opinion, threats near its borders, refugee inflows from Syria's ongoing conflict, and dependence on neighboring countries' energy sources (including Russia and Iran) have complicated its efforts to transcend the region's political, ethnic, and sectarian divides. In 2010, Turkey's fallout with Israel over the Gaza flotilla incident[8] and its vote (in concert with Brazil) against U.N. Security Council sanctions on Iran put it at odds with the United States on two key regional U.S. priorities.

Subsequent efforts to focus U.S.-Turkey regional cooperation on the post-conflict attempt to rehabilitate Iraq and on political transition in Arab countries beset by turmoil since 2010-2011 have been challenged by Turkey's geographic proximity to conflict areas and apparent interest in working with other actors espousing an overtly Sunni Muslim perspective. The idea of Turkey as a "model" or example for Arab countries to follow, though still significantly popular according to polling, appears to have less currency now.[9] This may be in part because Islamist movements that Erdogan and Davutoglu appeared to favor lost control of Egypt's government to the military in July 2013, and gradually lost control of the Syrian opposition to more extreme Islamist groups. Turkey's internal political controversies since June 2013—as portrayed in regional and international media—may have also reduced its appeal to neighboring countries.[10]

Despite some challenges to U.S.-Turkey cooperation, the two countries appear to work frequently to bring their policies closer together. Agreement by Turkey in 2011 to host a U.S. early warning radar as part of a nascent NATO Active Layered Theater Ballistic Missile Defense (ALTBMD)

---

[6] See, e.g., Ahmet Davutoglu, "Principles of Turkish Foreign Policy and Regional Political Structuring," International Policy and Leadership Institute and Economic Policy Research Foundation of Turkey (TEPAV), Turkey Policy Brief Series, 2012 – Third Edition.

[7] See, e.g., Council on Foreign Relations, *U.S.-Turkey Relations: A New Partnership*, Madeleine K. Albright and Steven J. Hadley, Co-Chairs, Independent Task Force Report No. 69, 2012, p. 40.

[8] The incident took place in May 2010 in international waters under disputed circumstances and resulted in the death of eight Turks and an American of Turkish descent. It was predated by other signs of deterioration in Turkey's relationship with Israel.

[9] Sevgi Akarcesme, "Turkey's approval rating in Middle East down 10 percent from 2012," *Today's Zaman*, December 3, 2013. Arab interpretations of the "Turkish model" tend to emphasize the recent democratic and economic empowerment of Turkey's middle class and the connection between this and Turkey's emergence as a regional power with a foreign policy independent of the West. Many analysts and Turkish officials have stated that Turkey might more aptly be characterized as an inspiration than as a model because the historical experiences and characteristics of its people, society, and economic system are distinct from those of Arab countries.

[10] See, e.g., Tim Arango, "Turkey, Its Allies Struggling, Tempers Ambitions to Lead Region," *New York Times*, November 21, 2013.

---

system for Europe[11] went some way toward addressing U.S. questions about Turkey's alignment with the West on the Iranian nuclear issue. Similarly, after the manifestation of U.S.-Turkey differences on various other issues, the Obama Administration has made repeated efforts to clarify U.S. priorities, and Turkey has in many cases publicly indicated an effort to move closer to U.S. positions or to deemphasize points of disagreement.[12] Such cases include:

- Turkish leaders' statements indicating plans to improve their troubled relations with Israel.[13]

- Turkey's reported reconsideration of its provisional decision in September 2013 to co-produce a long-range air and missile defense system with a Chinese government-owned company, rather than with a U.S. or European partner.[14]

- Apparent Turkish efforts to increase scrutiny of and controls on Syrian oppositionists and foreign fighters/jihadists traversing Turkish territory. These efforts may get added impetus with the Islamic State's (also known as Islamic State of Iraq and the Levant, or ISIL) recent territorial gains in Iraq and taking of Turkish hostages.[15]

- A diplomatic initiative renewed in early 2014 to move toward greater normalization, if not a definitive resolution, between ethnic Turks and ethnic Greeks in Cyprus.

- Prime Minister Erdogan's speech in April 2014, containing some seemingly conciliatory statements, regarding World War I-era actions by the Ottoman Empire against Armenians that are characterized by many countries as genocide.[16]

---

[11] The proposed elements of the European Phased Adaptive Approach (EPAA) to missile defense proposed by the Obama Administration, which represents the U.S. contribution to NATO's ALTBMD system, and a deployment timeline were described in a September 15, 2011, White House press release available at http://www.whitehouse.gov/the-press-office/2011/09/15/fact-sheet-implementing-missile-defense-europe. This document explicitly contemplates the EPAA as a means of countering missile threats from Iran. Then Deputy Assistant Secretary of State for Arms Control, Verification and Compliance Frank Rose gave a speech in Warsaw, Poland, on April 18, 2013 (available at http://www.state.gov/t/avc/rls/2013/207679 htm), that described how the EPAA has been implemented and revised. See also CRS Report RL34051, *Long-Range Ballistic Missile Defense in Europe*, by Steven A. Hildreth and Carl Ek.

[12] See, e.g., Ali H. Aslan, "Zero Problems with the US?," *Today's Zaman*, November 17, 2013.

[13] Aron Donzis, "Turkish PM: Rapprochement with Israel coming in weeks," *Times of Israel*, April 29, 2014. However, these prospects may change in light of the July 2014 Israel-Gaza conflict, heightened Turkish criticism of Israel, and possible Turkish political mediation on behalf of Hamas (with which Turkey has maintained positive relations for several years). Partial transcript of Prime Minister Erdogan's interview with CNN's Becky Anderson, July 23, 2014, available at http://cnnpressroom.blogs.cnn.com/2014/07/23/turkish-pm-erdogan-to-cnn-israel-is-a-terror-state/.

[14] Denise Der, "Why Turkey May Not Buy Chinese Missile Systems After All," *Diplomat*, May 7, 2014.

[15] Joe Parkinson and Emre Peker, "Iraq Hostages Show Turkey's Exposure in Violent Region," *Wall Street Journal*,

[16] Translated text of statement available at http://www hurriyetdailynews.com/turkish-pm-erdogans-april-23-statement-on-armenian-issue-in-english.aspx?pageID=238&nID=65454&NewsCatID=359. Erdogan made this speech on April 23, the eve of Armenians' annual remembrance day for the events in question. On April 10, 2014, the Senate Foreign Relations Committee had favorably reported S.Res. 410 ("A resolution expressing the sense of the Senate regarding the anniversary of the Armenian Genocide.").

Strategic Assessment

Turkey's leaders may be at least partly motivated to minimize disagreement with the United States and other actors in order to improve their domestic profiles and ease international scrutiny amid current election season controversies. Turkey's dependence on foreign energy and capital might also be a factor. The resolution or mitigation of disputes involving Cyprus, Armenia, and Israel might increase Western support for an Eastern Mediterranean pipeline from Israel's and Cyprus's offshore natural fields to Turkey[17]—perhaps as part of a larger effort to find alternatives for Europe to Russian-origin energy sources. Turkish leaders might also be trying to boost external investor confidence in its markets and to improve prospects of being included directly or indirectly in the possible negotiation of a U.S.-European Union Transatlantic Trade and Investment Partnership (TTIP).

However, patterns in the U.S.-Turkey bilateral relationship also suggest that periodic miscommunications and divergences in their respective interests may persist. For example, Turkey appears to be aiding Iraq's Kurdish Regional Government in its efforts to export oil through Turkey without the approval of Iraq's central government, which U.S. officials have reportedly asserted could further undermine Iraq's already shaky political stability and sovereign unity. Turkey seems to be preparing for the possibility of a Kurdish state in northern Iraq in the wake of developments in Iraq since June 2014. Additionally, in late June, the House Foreign Affairs Committee reported the Turkey Christian Churches Accountability Act (H.R. 4347),[18] which prompted a negative reaction from Turkish officials.[19]

In light of recent U.S. responses to events in Syria, Iraq, and Ukraine, Turkey may be assessing how to gauge the likely nature and extent of U.S. involvement in current and future regional crises, and how that might shape its own regional approach. In July 2014, Erdogan indicated that he no longer speaks directly with President Obama, saying "Naturally because I did not get the results I wanted in this process, in particular on Syria, our foreign ministers hold talks, as I do with (U.S. Vice President Joe) Biden."[20] Turkey's unwillingness or inability to project force into Syria in the face of vulnerabilities it confronted from Syria's internal conflict appears to have increased Turkey's dependence on U.S. and NATO security guarantees and assistance, at least in the near term. Possible Turkish expectations of imminent U.S.-led military action in Syria appear to have dissipated with President Obama's acceptance in September 2013 of a U.N. Security Council-backed agreement regarding chemical weapons removal. For the time being on Syria and Iraq, given Turkey's military constraints and geographic sensitivities, it may anticipate influencing outcomes in its favor and minimizing vulnerabilities through political dealmaking with other regional and international actors—probably including Russia, Iran, Iraq's central government, the Asad regime, and various Kurdish groups.

---

[17] See, e.g., Deniz Arslan, "Erdoğan pledges new reforms amid mounting Western criticism on rights," *todayszaman.com*, May 4, 2014.

[18] Sponsored by Edward Royce, Chairman of the House Foreign Affairs Committee, the bill would compel the Secretary of State to file an annual report on the status of Turkey's actions and the State Department's engagement with respect to the property claims of various Christian churches in Turkey and in the area of northern Cyprus that is de facto controlled by ethnic Turks.

[19] Julian Pecquet, "Turkey lashes out at Congress over Christian churches bill," *Al-Monitor Congress Pulse*, June 27, 2014.

[20] Gulsen Solaker, "Turkey's Erdogan acknowledges strains with Obama," *Reuters*, July 22, 2014.

Impact of Public Opinion, Debate, and Reaction

Public opinion may also affect Turkey's future relationship with the United States and NATO. According to a 2012 Council on Foreign Relations task force report co-chaired by former Secretary of State Madeleine Albright and former National Security Advisor Stephen Hadley (the "Albright-Hadley report"), "public opinion polls in Turkey consistently reveal unfavorable impressions of the United States among the Turkish public.... This is a problem that can damage the bilateral relations, especially now that public opinion matters more than ever before in Turkish foreign policy."[21] Such unfavorable impressions, to the extent they exist, do so within a context of Turks' generally low favorability ratings for foreign countries.[22] Many observers cite a "Sèvres syndrome"[23] among Turks historically wary of encirclement by neighboring and global powers—especially Westerners. On the subject of a possible "Armenian genocide resolution" in Congress (see "Possible "Armenian Genocide Resolution"" below), Turkish statements and actions in response to past Congressional action suggest that any future action would probably have at least some negative consequences for bilateral relations and defense cooperation in the short term—with long-term ramifications less clear.

Negative U.S. public reactions to Turkish statements, actions, and perceived double standards could also impact the bilateral relationship, as could reactions to developments in domestic politics (discussed below) that appear—in the words of two U.S.-based commentators (one of whom is a former U.S. ambassador to Turkey)—to harm the "century-long American effort to promote liberal universal values."[24] According to a Turkish newspaper report, Turkey's reported disclosure to Iran in 2011—in apparent retribution for the 2010 Gaza flotilla incident—of the identities of Iranians acting as Israeli intelligence sources led to Congressional rejection (presumably informal) of Turkey's longstanding request to purchase U.S. drone aircraft to counter Kurdish militants.[25] Additionally, Obama Administration officials reportedly harbor concerns regarding conspiratorial insinuations in circles close to Erdogan about alleged U.S. or international efforts to stir up recent domestic controversies.[26] Moreover, Administration officials and Members of Congress have criticized negative statements about Israel, Zionism, and

---

[21] Council on Foreign Relations, op. cit., p. 7. Other prominent reports on U.S.-Turkey relations in recent years include an October 2013 report by the Bipartisan Policy Center that was co-chaired by former U.S. ambassadors to Turkey Morton Abramowitz and Eric Edelman, op. cit., and a 2011 report by the Istanbul-based Global Relations Forum. Global Relations Forum, *Turkey-USA Partnership: At the Dawn of a New Century*, Co-Chairs Fusun Turkmen and Yavuz Canevi.

[22] The Pew Research Global Attitudes Project indicates that 21% of Turks polled in 2013 had a favorable opinion of the United States, up from 10% in 2011. However, unlike citizens polled from other Muslim-majority countries in the region who had a significantly more favorable opinion of China than the United States, Turks' favorability of China was only six percentage points higher (27%). Poll results available at http://www.pewglobal.org/2013/07/18/americas-global-image-remains-more-positive-than-chinas/.

[23] Dietrich Jung, "Sèvres Syndrome: Turkish Foreign Policy and Its Historical Legacies," *American Diplomacy*, August 2003; Transatlantic Academy Scholars Views on Turkish Public Opinion, October 1, 2009. This refers to the Treaty of Sèvres agreed to in 1920 (but not ratified) by the defeated Ottoman Empire with the Allied victors of World War I. The Treaty of Sèvres would have partitioned the Empire among Britain, France, Italy, Greece, and Armenia. The treaty became obsolete with the Turkish War of Independence and the subsequent Treaty of Lausanne in 1923, which formalized the borders of the new Turkish Republic.

[24] Soner Cagaptay and James F. Jeffrey, "Turkey's 2014 Political Transition: From Erdogan to Erdogan?," Washington Institute for Near East Policy, Policy Notes No. 17, January 2014.

[25] "Report: US canceled delivery of Predators to Turkey," *Today's Zaman*, October 21, 2013, citing a report in *Taraf*.

[26] Scott Peterson, "Why President Obama stopped calling Turkish leader Erdogan," *Christian Science Monitor*, March 7, 2014.

---

apparently in some cases broader groups of Jewish people by Erdogan or other Turkish leaders in relation to the flotilla incident, Israel's treatment of Palestinians (including during the July 2014 Israel-Gaza conflict), a February 2013 international conference in Vienna, Turkey's June 2013 domestic protests,[27] and Egypt's July 2013 military takeover. This is exacerbated by Turkey's cultivation of ties with Hamas and refusal to characterize it as a terrorist organization.

The optics of the proposed missile defense deal with CPMIEC, due both to U.S. public sensitivities regarding China and to CPMIEC's subjection to U.S. sanctions for alleged proliferation-related dealings with certain countries,[28] could further complicate the public dimension of U.S.-Turkey relations. The deal may be even more problematic given that it could be interpreted as a rejection of the very U.S. Patriot missile defense batteries that are currently deployed under NATO auspices at Turkey's request to defend it from threats in Syria.

It remains unclear how trends or fluctuations in public opinion—when taken together with how the countries' leaders cooperate on strategic matters and with other factors such as trade, tourism, and cultural and educational exchange—will affect the tenor of the U.S.-Turkey relationship over the long term.

Bilateral and NATO Defense Cooperation[29]

Overview

The U.S.-Turkey alliance has long centered on the defense relationship, both bilaterally and within NATO. Turkey's location near several global hotspots makes the continuing availability of its territory for the stationing and transport of arms, cargo, and personnel valuable for the United States and NATO. Turkey also controls access to and from the Black Sea through its straits pursuant to the Montreux Convention of 1936. Turkey's hosting of a U.S./NATO early warning missile defense radar and the transformation of a NATO air command unit in Izmir into a ground forces command appear to have reinforced Turkey's strategic importance for the alliance. For information on NATO's role in supporting Turkey's defense in light of ongoing conflict in Syria, see "Syria" below.

As the military's political influence within Turkey has declined, civilian leaders have assumed primary responsibility for national security decisions. Changes in the Turkish power structure present a challenge for U.S. officials accustomed to military interlocutors in adjusting future modes of bilateral interaction. It might lead to an approach that is more multidimensional than the

---

[27] According to the State Department's International Religious Freedom Report for 2013, "In June and July, in response to the Gezi Park anti-government protests, Prime Minister Erdogan and several senior government officials repeatedly and publicly blamed 'shadowy' international groups for the unrest, including claimed involvement by an 'international Jewish conspiracy,' the 'interest-rate lobby,' and 'the Rothschilds.' In July Deputy Prime Minister Besir Atalay blamed the 'Jewish diaspora' for the unrest. These statements by senior political leaders were accompanied by anti-Semitic reports and commentaries in media outlets friendly to the government. The chief rabbi and the Jewish community lay board issued a joint press release condemning statements blaming Jewish groups for the unrest."

[28] CRS Report RL31555, *China and Proliferation of Weapons of Mass Destruction and Missiles: Policy Issues*, by Shirley A. Kan.

[29] For background information on this subject, see archived CRS Report R41761, *Turkey-U.S. Defense Cooperation: Prospects and Challenges*, by Jim Zanotti.

well-established pattern some observers see in which the State Department and other U.S. officials rely on the "Pentagon to wield its influence."[30]

The largest U.S. military presence in Turkey is at Incirlik (pronounced *in-jur-lick*) air base near the southern city of Adana, with approximately 1,500 U.S. personnel (plus approximately 3,500 Turkish contractors). Since the end of the Cold War, Incirlik has been used to support U.S. and NATO operations in Iraq, Bosnia-Herzegovina, Kosovo, and Afghanistan. According to the *Bulletin of the Atomic Scientists*, Incirlik also is the reported home of vaults holding approximately 60-70 U.S. tactical, aircraft-deliverable B61 nuclear gravity bombs under NATO auspices.[31] Turkey maintains the right to cancel U.S. access to Incirlik with three days' notice.

---

[30] Henri J. Barkey, "Turkey's New Global Role," Carnegie Endowment for International Peace, November 17, 2010. The challenge for U.S. officials to manage cooperation with Turkey could be magnified by the way the U.S. government is structured to work with Turkey. Former U.S. ambassador to Turkey Mark Parris has written, "For reasons of self-definition and Cold War logic, Turkey is considered a European nation. It is therefore assigned, for purposes of policy development and implementation, to the subdivisions responsible for Europe: the European Bureau (EUR) at the State Department; the European Command (EUCOM) at the Pentagon; the Directorate for Europe at the [National Security Council (NSC)], etc. Since the end of the Cold War, however, and progressively since the 1990-91 Gulf War and 9/11, the most serious issues in U.S.-Turkish relations – and virtually all of the controversial ones – have arisen in areas outside "Europe." The majority, in fact, stem from developments in areas which in Washington are the responsibility of offices dealing with the Middle East: the Bureau for Near East Affairs (NEA) at State; Central Command (CENTCOM) at the Pentagon; the Near East and South Asia Directorate at NSC." Omer Taspinar, "The Rise of Turkish Gaullism: Getting Turkish-American Relations Right," *Insight Turkey*, vol. 13, no. 1, winter 2011, quoting an unpublished 2008 paper by Mark Parris.

[31] Robert S. Norris and Hans M. Kristensen, "US tactical nuclear weapons in Europe, 2011," *Bulletin of the Atomic Scientists*, vol. 67, no. 1, January/February 2011. Reportedly, the U.S. has approximately 150-200 B61 bombs in Turkey, Belgium, Germany, Italy, and the Netherlands left over from their deployment during the Cold War. This amount is a very small fraction of the over 7,000 U.S. tactical nuclear weapons stationed in Europe during the 1970s. Ibid.

Figure 2. Map of U.S. and NATO Military Presence in Turkey

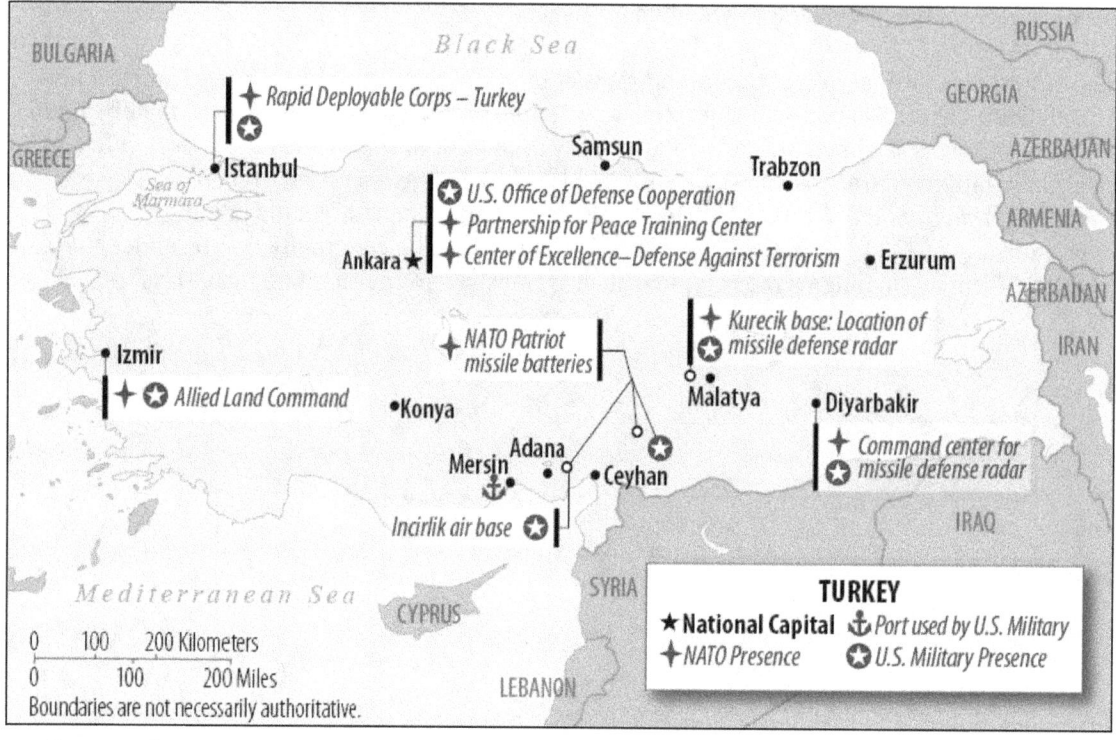

Sources: Department of Defense, NATO, *Hurriyet Daily News*; adapted by CRS.

Notes: All locations are approximate. The Incirlik and Kurecik bases are Turkish bases, parts of which are used for limited purposes by the U.S. military and NATO. Additional information on the U.S./NATO military presence in Turkey is available in archived CRS Report R41761, *Turkey-U.S. Defense Cooperation: Prospects and Challenges*, by Jim Zanotti.

Since 1948, the United States has provided Turkey with approximately $13.8 billion in overall military assistance (nearly $8.2 billion in grants and $5.6 billion in loans). Current annual military and security grant assistance, however, is limited to approximately $4-5 million annually in International Military Education and Training (IMET); and Nonproliferation, Antiterrorism, Demining and Related Programs (NADR) funds (see **Table 4** below).

Afghanistan

Turkey has twice commanded the International Security Assistance Force (ISAF) in Afghanistan and has had troops participating in ISAF since shortly after its inception in December 2001. Turkey's approximately 2,000 troops concentrate on training Afghan military and security forces and providing security in Kabul, where Turkey commands ISAF's Regional Command-Capital, as well as in Wardak (just west of Kabul) and Jawzjan (in northern Afghanistan) provinces. In addition, some Afghan police are trained in Turkey.

As with several other NATO and non-NATO contributors to ISAF, Turkey's troops are not involved in combat. Turkey's history of good relations with both Afghanistan and Pakistan and its status as the Muslim-majority country with the greatest level of involvement in ISAF are thought by some analysts to help legitimize ISAF's presence. These relations could become more important to preparing Afghanistan for self-rule, with the United States and other ISAF countries scheduled to wind down their military presence in Afghanistan in the near future.

China-Turkey Air and Missile Defense Cooperation?

Turkey's leaders openly speak of desires to strengthen the country's self-sufficiency—including in military and technological capacity. That may partly explain Turkey's announced but unfinalized September 2013 decision to develop the multi-billion dollar long-range air and missile Turkish Long Range Air and Missile Defense System (T-LORAMIDS) with a Chinese government-owned company (CPMIEC, or the China Precision Machinery Import and Export Corporation) that is offering relatively favorable co-production and technology sharing terms in comparison with competing U.S. and European offers. It is unclear whether, over the long term, political and operational considerations will allow Turkey to expect continued or improved protection from NATO's ALTBMD architecture if it acquires an independent, non-interoperable capacity in close cooperation with a potential U.S. rival.[32] In considering the potential missile defense deal, some Western observers are revisiting questions about Turkey's long-term commitment to NATO.[33] Nevertheless, shortly following the decision, Turkish President Abdullah Gul stated that the CPMIEC deal "is not definite. There is a shortlist, and China is at the top of it. We should look at the conditions, but there is no doubt that Turkey is primarily in NATO. These are multi-dimensional issues, there are technical and economic dimensions and on the other hand there is an alliance dimension. These are being evaluated."[34] As mentioned above, reports in 2014 have indicated that Turkey is reconsidering the deal and remains open to partnering with U.S. or European companies as an alternative to CPMIEC.

Turkey's 2009 request for outside tenders for an off-the-shelf version of T-LORAMIDS had been scrapped in January 2013 in favor of a version that would feature Turkish co-production of the system, in line with Turkey's general procurement policy favoring technology acquisition that can bolster its self-reliance. Murad Bayar, Turkey's top defense procurement official until early 2014, claimed that CPMIEC's offer of the HQ-9/FD-2000 system bested the competitors—including a U.S. Raytheon/Lockheed-Martin offer of a Patriot PAC-3 system and bids from Italian/French and Russian contractors—on the basis of price, co-production, and technology transfer criteria. Despite initial expectations that the deal would be finalized in the first half of 2014, it was not, and, as mentioned above, it is possible that Turkey is leaving the door open to U.S. and European offers.

It is unclear to what extent U.S. bidders or U.S. officials are considering ways to persuade Turkey to change its decision. Seven Senators sent a letter dated October 11, 2013, to Secretary of State John Kerry and Secretary of Defense Chuck Hagel, urging them to "exert all available diplomatic pressure to prevent Turkish procurement of a CPMIEC missile defense system and ensure NATO will never allow such a system to be integrated into NATO's security architecture," and to "undertake a comprehensive review of the security implications posed by this procurement and report back with appropriate steps the U.S. and NATO should take to protect the security of classified data and technology."[35] A letter raising similar concerns about the proposed deal was

---

[32] See, e.g., Nilsu Goren, "Turkey's Air and Missile Defense Acquisition Journey Continues," EDAM (Centre for Economics and Foreign Policy Studies), Discussion Paper Series 2013/13, October 2013.

[33] See, e.g., Daniel Dombey, "Doubts rise over Turkey's ties to the West," *Financial Times*, October 20, 2013. In April 2013, Turkey became a "dialogue partner" with the China- and Russia-led Shanghai Cooperation Organization (SCO). Turkey is the only NATO member with a formal affiliation with the SCO, though it does not appear to have significant influence with the organization.

[34] "Turkey's China deal on missile system not finalized, says President Gül," *Hurriyet Daily News*, September 30, 2013.

[35] The Senators are Mark Kirk, John Cornyn, Roger Wicker, John Barrasso, John Boozman, James Inhofe, and Ted (continued...)

sent on November 4, 2013, to Turkey's then U.S. ambassador Namik Tan by House Armed Services Committee Chairman Howard "Buck" McKeon and Ranking Member Adam Smith.[36] In the event that the CPMIEC deal is finalized, Chinese personnel would likely receive significantly greater access—including for purposes of training and consultation—to officials and organizations associated with Turkey's security establishment and defense industry.

The announcement of the possible Turkey-CPMIEC deal prompted reactions of surprise and concern from Western observers. U.S. and NATO officials, while acknowledging Turkey's right to make its own procurement decisions, have claimed that the Chinese system would not be interoperable with NATO air and missile defense assets—including radar sensors—in Turkey. Although two U.S.-based analysts maintain that interoperability may be technically possible, they assert that "Turkey's allies would make the political decision not to allow full integration," taking into account the "potential risk of Chinese infiltration or exfiltration of data."[37] In response to the announced possible Turkey-CPMIEC deal, Senator Mark Kirk proposed S.Amdt. 2287 to the National Defense Authorization Act for Fiscal Year 2014 (incorporated into H.R. 3304, which was enacted as P.L. 113-66), which prohibits any U.S. funding to be used to "integrate missile defense systems of the People's Republic of China into United States missile defense systems." One analyst asserts that lack of NATO interoperability could make the CPMIEC offer significantly less cost-advantageous for Turkey in the long run.[38]

U.S. officials have additionally emphasized that CPMIEC is subject to U.S. sanctions under the Iran, North Korea and Syria Nonproliferation Act (P.L. 106-178, as amended).[39] One media report cited an unnamed U.S. diplomat as saying that Turkish companies involved in co-production with CPMIEC "would be denied access to any use of US technology or equipment in relation to this program," and as suggesting that such companies might also face difficulties in working with U.S. products or technology on other projects.[40] The diplomat reportedly compared this situation with difficulties that the United States encountered in the past decade-and-a-half with Israel when it sold drone aircraft to China.[41] A *Reuters* article said that "Turkey's missile defense deal could also affect its plans to buy radar-evading F-35 fighter jets" from the United States.[42]

In defending Turkey's decision to engage in co-production with a non-NATO country, Erdogan has referenced NATO member Greece's previous procurement of a missile defense system from Russia (another non-NATO country). Additionally, Turkey reportedly cooperated with China

---

(...continued)

Cruz. A copy of the signed letter was provided to CRS by a Congressional office on December 13, 2013. The letter states that if Turkey procures the CPMIEC system, possible responses could include "Turkish expulsion from the NATO Air Defense Ground Environment and intensified scrutiny of all Turkey-NATO security cooperation activities."

[36] A copy of the signed letter was provided to CRS by a Congressional office on December 13, 2013.

[37] Bulent Aliriza and Samuel J. Brannen, "Turkey Looks to China on Air and Missile Defense?," Center for Strategic and International Studies, October 8, 2013.

[38] Aaron Stein, "More thoughts on Turkey and Missile Defense Decision-Making," *Turkey Wonk*, November 25, 2013.

[39] CRS Report RL31555, *China and Proliferation of Weapons of Mass Destruction and Missiles: Policy Issues*, by Shirley A. Kan.

[40] Burak Ege Bekdil, "Turk Industry Could Face US Sanctions in China Air Defense Deal," *Defense News*, November 19, 2013.

[41] Ibid. See also CRS Report RL33476, *Israel: Background and U.S. Relations*, by Jim Zanotti.

[42] Andrea Shalal-Esa, "Turkey asks U.S. to extend pricing on Raytheon missile bid: sources," *Reuters*, October 28, 2013.

---

decades ago in connection with a ballistic missile program.[43] One report claims that the Turkish military is unhappy that it might acquire "second-hand, not battle-tested and cheap Chinese missiles," while also claiming that the military is "mad" because U.S. companies did not offer more generous technology transfer terms.[44] President Gul's statement (cited above) insisting that the deal "is not definite" and that "Turkey is primarily in NATO"[45] hints at an apparent awareness that U.S./NATO scrutiny of the possible deal probably considers its overall context. This includes potential Western geopolitical rivalry with China, Turkey's greater assertiveness on the international stage, and other steps—perhaps tentative and inconclusive—that Turkey and China have taken to bolster political, military, and trade ties.[46] Additionally, the McKeon-Smith letter asserts that Turkey's pursuit of a deal with CPMIEC seems to undermine its commitment to NATO burden sharing, "even as Turkey would benefit from the defense capabilities of those states which have deployed their own assets on Turkey's soil to defend the Turkish people."[47]

In addition to raising questions about Turkey's overall foreign policy goals and relationships, it is unclear what a CPMIEC missile defense deal would mean for Turkey's defense posture. Is Turkey seeking a system that could cover potential territorial gaps in NATO's ALTBMD coverage? Is it seeking a system that offers redundant or alternative protection in the event that NATO coverage is technically deficient, or in the event that Turkey's association with NATO provokes an unacceptable level of regional threat? Does Turkey question the political will of other NATO countries to come to its defense and stay engaged in the event of a conflict featuring missile exchanges? Or is the Turkish decision on CPMIEC confined to the specific details of the transaction with negligible connection to larger geopolitical or operational objectives?

Country Overview

Since the 1980s, Turkey has experienced fundamental internal change—particularly the economic empowerment of a middle class from its Anatolian heartland that emphasizes Sunni Muslim values. This change has helped fuel continuing political transformation led in the past decade by Prime Minister Erdogan, President Gul, and Foreign Minister Davutoglu (all of whom are profiled in **Appendix A**). They all come from the Islamic-leaning AKP, which first came to power in elections in 2002. For decades, the Turkish republic relied upon its military, judiciary, and other bastions of its Kemalist (a term inspired by Turkey's republican founder, Mustafa Kemal

---

[43] Tulin Daloglu, "Turkey, China cooperation on ballistic missiles not new," *Al-Monitor Turkey Pulse*, December 13, 2013.

[44] Lale Kemal, "Turkish military very unhappy with Chinese missiles, mad at US," *Today's Zaman*, November 5, 2013.

[45] "Turkey's China deal on missile system not finalized, says President Gül," *Hurriyet Daily News*, September 30, 2013.

[46] Although such steps have taken place, including the increase of bilateral trade volume to around $24 billion (from $1 billion in 2000), some degree of tension between Turkey and China persists over the imbalance of trade between the two countries (in China's favor), as well as over Turkey's concerns regarding China's treatment of Uighurs (who are ethnically and linguistically akin to Turks) in its Xinjiang Province. Turkish and Chinese military units held joint air and ground exercises in Turkey during 2010, but have apparently not done so since. One project showcasing increased Turkey-China commercial relations is the involvement of two Chinese companies in the construction of a key section of an Istanbul-Ankara high-speed railway that began operating in July 2014. For additional information on the dynamics of the Turkey-China relationship, see Karen Kaya, "Turkey and China: Unlikely Strategic Partners," Foreign Military Studies Office (Fort Leavenworth, Kansas), August 2013; and Chris Zambelis, "Sino-Turkish Partnership: Implications of Anatolian Eagle 2010," *China Brief*, vol. 11, no. 1, January 2011.

[47] See footnote 36.

Ataturk) "secular elite" to protect it from political and ideological extremes—sacrificing at least some of its democratic vitality in the process. Through a series of elections, popular referenda, court decisions, and other political developments within the existing constitutional order, Turkey has changed into a more civilian-led system that increasingly reflects the new middle class's dedication to market economics and conservative values.

Table 1. Parties in Turkey's Parliament

(Based on national elections held in June 2011)

Party	June 2011 Vote	Members of Parliament	General Orientation
Justice and Development Party (AKP) Leader: Recep Tayyip Erdogan	49.8%	318	Economic liberalism, social conservatism
Republican People's Party (CHP) Leader: Kemal Kilicdaroglu	26.0%	134	Social democracy, secularist interests
Nationalist Action Party (MHP) Leader: Devlet Bahceli	13.0%	52	Turkish nationalist interests
Peoples' Democratic Party (HDP) Co-Leaders: Selahattin Demirtas and Figen Yuksekdag	6.6%[a]	30	Ethnic Kurdish interests, social democracy

Sources: Turkish Grand National Assembly website; Ali Carkoglu, "Turkey's 2011 General Elections: Towards a Dominant Party System?" *Insight Turkey*, vol. 13, no. 3, summer 2011, pp. 43-62.

Note: There are 14 nominally independent members of parliament, some of whom are associated with the BDP, and some of whom were formerly members of other parties.

a. This is the percentage vote figure for the 61 BDP members or affiliated individuals who ran in the election as independents for individual geographic constituencies, as described in footnote 93.

As discussed above, Turkey's internal transformation has helped to drive increased engagement and influence within its own region and internationally. At the same time, its leaders have tried to maintain Turkey's traditional alliances and economic partnerships with Western nations in NATO and the EU, routinely asserting that Turkey's location at the crossroads of Europe and Asia and its soft power provides it and its allies with "strategic depth." Thus, the geopolitical importance of Turkey for the United States is now intertwined with its importance as an ally and symbol— politically, culturally, economically, and religiously. Turkey's future influence could depend on its maintaining the robust economic growth from its past decade that has led to its having the world's 17th-largest economy.

For additional historical context, see **Appendix C**.

Recent Domestic Controversies: Erdogan, the Fethullah Gulen Movement, and the Justice Sector

In mid-December 2013, a number of government ministers' sons and prominent businessmen close to Prime Minister Erdogan and other top Turkish officials were arrested on corruption-related charges. Since then, Turkey's domestic political situation has been tense and polarized. Erdogan himself has been implicated in questions of corruption and media interference and has used his office both to fend off potential threats to his position and stature and to weaken those who initiated or support the investigations. He now openly portrays the Fethullah Gulen movement, an influential civil society group that had largely made common cause with the AKP during its first decade in power (see textbox below), as his politically motivated opponents.

Fethullah Gulen Movement[48]

The Fethullah Gulen movement (or community) is a multifaceted array of individuals and organizations in Turkey and other countries around the world. This apparently includes schools[49] and other organizations[50] located in the United States. Such individuals and organizations tend to subscribe to or sympathize with the teachings of Fethullah Gulen, a former Turkish state imam who is now a permanent U.S. resident.[51] The Gulen movement became a Turkey-wide grassroots movement in the 1980s as part of the emergence of the new conservative Turkish middle class. Gulen preaches a distinctly Turkish brand of Islam that condemns terrorism,[52] promotes interfaith dialogue and cross-cultural understanding, and can function in concert with secular democratic mechanisms and modern economic and technological modes of living.

There is widespread speculation that Gulen movement adherents or sympathizers occupy influential positions within Turkey's civil service.[53] Gulen and his close supporters insist that in any event, he does not hierarchically control Turkish state employees or any others who, through their public or private activities, align themselves with him and his teachings.[54] This point is actively debated inside and outside of Turkey. [55]

---

[48] For a range of views on the Gulen movement, see Joshua D. Hendrick, *Gulen: The Ambiguous Politics of Market Islam in Turkey and the World*, New York: New York University Press, 2013; M. Hakan Yavuz, *Toward an Islamic Enlightenment: The Gulen Movement*, New York: Oxford University Press, 2013; Helen Rose Ebaugh, *The Gulen Movement: A Sociological Analysis of a Civic Movement Rooted in Moderate Islam*, New York: Springer, 2010; "Hank, The Gulen Movement, The Role of a Lifetime," *60 Minutes*, CBS News, May 13, 2012; Alexander Brock, "What Is the Gulen Movement?," Council on Foreign Relations, op. cit., Appendix B; Claire Berlinski, "Who Is Fethullah Gulen?," *City Journal*, vol. 22, no. 4, autumn 2012.

[49] Gulen-inspired organizations have reportedly founded and operate approximately 136 publicly funded charter schools in 26 U.S. states. Hendrick, op. cit., p. 217. These schools have generated publicity both for their high academic quality and for questions, legal and state regulatory action, and possible federal investigations regarding their hiring and business practices and local approvals processes. Stephanie Saul, "Charter Schools Tied to Turkey Grow in Texas," *New York Times*, June 6, 2011; Martha Woodall, "Ex-teacher, school settle bias case," *philly.com*, May 14, 2013; Dan Mihalopoulos, "CPS says no to charter schools, but state commission says yes," *suntimes.com*, December 23, 2013; Danielle Nadler, "School Board Rejects Charter School," *leesburgtoday.com* (Loudoun County, VA), February 28, 2013; Elizabeth Stuart, "Islamic links to Utah's Beehive Academy probed," *Deseret News*, June 1, 2010. In 2011, a New Orleans school that some reports had linked to the Gulen movement was shut down—reportedly over an alleged bribery attempt—and a school in Baton Rouge overseen by the same foundation is reportedly the subject to an FBI inquiry. Diana Samuels, "Kenilworth charter school, subject of apparent FBI inquiry, has ties to Turkish education movement," *Times-Picayune* (New Orleans), December 12, 2013. Tennessee's legislature passed a 2012 bill limiting the percentage of foreign employees permitted to work in its charter schools. The initiative was reportedly driven in large part by political activists citing various media reports on Gulen-inspired schools. Mark Todd Engler, "Legislature Passes Limits on Foreign Staffers at TN Charter Schools," *tnreport.com*, April 16, 2012.

[50] Adherents of Gulen's teachings are involved with Turkish and Turkish-American trade associations and foundations active in the United States—both regionally and in the Washington, DC, area. Such organizations reportedly include the Turkic American Alliance umbrella of organizations and the business confederation TUSKON. Ilhan Tanir, "The Gulen movement plays big in Washington," *Hurriyet Daily News*, May 14, 2010; Ebaugh, op. cit., p. 49.

[51] Gulen lives in seclusion at a retreat center with a few of his adherents in Saylorsburg, PA, in the Pocono Mountains. He came to the United States in the late 1990s for medical treatment for a cardiovascular condition, and elected to stay after an ultimately unsuccessful criminal case was brought against him in Turkey charging that he sought to undermine Turkey's secular government.

[52] Days after the Al Qaeda terrorist attacks on September 11, 2011, Gulen took out an advertisement in the *Washington Post* condemning the attacks as incompatible with the teachings of Islam.

[53] Alexander Brock, "What Is the Gulen Movement?," Council on Foreign Relations, op. cit., Appendix B. The criminal case charging Gulen with undermining Turkey's secular government, which was dismissed in 2006, was largely based on a video in which Gulen apparently stated: "You must move in the arteries of the system without anyone noticing your existence until you reach all the power centers.... You must wait until such time as you have gotten all the state power, until you have brought to your side all the power of the constitutional institution in Turkey." Berlinski, op. cit. Many of Gulen's supporters claimed that the video had been doctored.

[54] "Turkey's Fethullah Gulen denies corruption probe links," *BBC News*, January 27, 2014; "GYV: Hizmet a civilian movement, has no political ambitions," *Today's Zaman*, April 5, 2012.

Many observers characterize the movement as having used its social connectedness, international reach, and media clout[56] to ally itself with the Erdogan-led AKP—particularly during the AKP's first decade in power, as both groups sought to curb the military's control over civilian politics. The Erdogan-Gulen movement relationship has since undergone a significant reversal, as discussed elsewhere in this report.[57] Many of the movement's adherents and sympathizers have been among the most vocal supporters of the Ergenekon and Sledgehammer (*Balyoz*) prosecutions and convictions, which deal with alleged military-centered networks and plots aimed at overthrowing or undermining the AKP government.[58] It is unclear that either the AKP or the Gulen movement has viable substitutes to fill the roles that each has previously played in support of the other.[59] Gulen insists that he does not ally himself with specific political parties or candidates, but rather advocates for his supporters to back leaders who embody "values of democracy, universal human rights and freedoms."[60]

It remains unclear how these developments will ultimately impact Erdogan's hold on the government and overall legacy, or Turkey's relations with the United States or the European Union.

Although four government ministers subject to the initial corruption-related investigations resigned in late December 2013,[61] Erdogan has portrayed the investigations as a "dirty plot" controlled by the Fethullah Gulen movement. He and many domestic and international observers say that they believe the Gulen movement has significant influence over civil servants within the criminal justice sector who are movement adherents or sympathizers. Because Erdogan and his supporters in government and the media assert that some of these civil servants act in a way that

---

(...continued)

[55] For a range of views on the Gulen movement, see Joshua D. Hendrick, *Gulen: The Ambiguous Politics of Market Islam in Turkey and the World*, New York: New York University Press, 2013; M. Hakan Yavuz, *Toward an Islamic Enlightenment: The Gulen Movement*, New York: Oxford University Press, 2013; Helen Rose Ebaugh, *The Gulen Movement: A Sociological Analysis of a Civic Movement Rooted in Moderate Islam*, New York: Springer, 2010; "Hank, The Gulen Movement, The Role of a Lifetime," *60 Minutes*, CBS News, May 13, 2012; Alexander Brock, "What Is the Gulen Movement?," Council on Foreign Relations, op. cit., Appendix B; Claire Berlinski, "Who Is Fethullah Gulen?," *City Journal*, vol. 22, no. 4, autumn 2012

[56] Gulen-inspired businesses, media enterprises, schools, charitable organizations, and civil society groups now exercise considerable influence in Turkey. For example, adherents of Gulen's teachings launched the *Zaman* newspaper in 1986. It is now the most widely circulated newspaper in Turkey, and has an English-language sister publication, *Today's Zaman*. Gulen also encouraged a group of businessmen to launch the Samanyolu television channel—today a major channel in Turkey with a worldwide reach through satellite and Internet transmission—in 1993.

[57] One Turkish journalist, in attempting to contrast the Gulen movement with Islamists who supposedly have influence on the AKP, wrote, "The Gulen Movement, though it is pious and unmistakably Muslim, has always steered clear of Islamist ideology. Unlike the Islamists, who constitute an influential strain within the A.K.P., Mr. Gulen's followers have always valued Turkey's relations with the West, championed accession to the European Union, and have been friendly toward Jews and Christians. In return, some paranoid Turkish Islamists (and even some secular nationalists) have accused Mr. Gulen of being a 'C.I.A. agent.'" Mustafa Akyol, "More Divisions, More Democracy," *New York Times*, December 11, 2013.

[58] This probably at least partly owes to concerns about societal power dynamics and Gulen movement adherents' and sympathizers' perceptions of vulnerability, justice, and/or retribution involving the military and other guardians of Turkey's secular elite. Such concerns probably largely stem from the past imprisonment and prosecution of Fethullah Gulen under military-guided governments.

[59] See, e.g., Bayram Balci, "Turkey's Gülen Movement: Between Social Activism and Politics," Carnegie Endowment for International Peace, October 24, 2013; Piotr Zalewski, "Turkey's Erdogan Battles Country's Most Powerful Religious Movement," *time.com*, December 4, 2013.

[60] Joe Parkinson and Jay Solomon, "Fethullah Gulen's interview with The Wall Street Journal in English," *wsj.com*, January 21, 2014.

[61] The resignations took place as part of a larger cabinet reshuffle that was portrayed as preparation for the March 2014 elections and beyond. In resigning as environment and urban planning minister on December 25 in connection with the corruption investigations, Erdogan Bayraktar called on Prime Minister Erdogan to resign, claiming that the prime minister had approved many of the zoning plans targeted in the investigations.

---

places the Gulen movement's interests over that of the state's constitutionally selected representatives, Erdogan has taken to referring to the movement as the "parallel state" or "structure."

Erdogan Government and Gulen Movement: From Collaboration to Opposition: Timeline of Selected Events

November 2002	AKP comes to power in parliamentary elections.
March 2003	AKP co-founder Recep Tayyip Erdogan elected to parliament in special election; becomes prime minister.
April 2007	In the midst of parliamentary deliberations to elect a president, Turkey's military posts a statement on its website proclaiming its willingness to act to protect Turkey's secular system.
June 2007	Ergenekon criminal investigations regarding alleged "deep-state" network begin.
July 2007	AKP reelected in parliamentary elections with an increased percentage of the vote.
August 2007	AKP co-founder Abdullah Gul elected president by parliament.
October 2007	AKP successfully passes constitutional amendments in referendum.
July 2008	AKP survives closure case in Constitutional Court.
May 2010	*Mavi Marmara* (aka Gaza flotilla) incident publicly exposes apparent differences between Erdogan and Fethullah Gulen over the management of Turkey's international relations, particularly with Israel.
September 2010	AKP successfully passes constitutional amendments in referendum.
June 2011	AKP reelected in parliamentary elections with nearly 50% of the vote.
February 2012	Public prosecutor seeks to question current and former officials from National Intelligence Organization (MIT) regarding possible dealings with the Kurdistan Workers' Party (PKK); prosecutorial request is blocked after Erdogan-backed law passes parliament requiring prime ministerial consent; prosecutor and some police personnel are reassigned; many observers assert that the prosecutorial actions are influenced by the Gulen movement.
September 2012	Sledgehammer (*Balyoz*) verdicts regarding alleged coup plot convict more than 300 active and former military officers (some of whom are later released on appeal).
June 2013	Nationwide "Gezi Park" protests and government response raise questions among domestic and international observers regarding Erdogan's leadership style and prospects, while he emphasizes his electoral mandate.
August 2013	Verdicts in main Ergenekon case convict more than 250 individuals (some of whom are later released pending a possible final outcome).
October 2013	Turkey's education minister announces a plan to eventually close or repurpose private tutoring centers (dershanes), which are foundational centers of activity and sources of support for the Gulen movement; pro-Gulen movement and third-party media challenge the propriety and legality of the plan.
December 2013	Corruption-related arrests target several figures close to the government and directly implicate four ministers, who later resign as part of a larger cabinet reshuffle; Erdogan characterizes the investigations as a "dirty plot" by the Gulen movement to undermine his rule and begins an apparently calculated effort to gain greater control over the criminal justice sector.
December 2013 - March 2014	Erdogan and his supporters on one hand, and individuals associated with or possibly associated with the Gulen movement on the other, apparently seek to undermine each other's public position through a variety of statements and actions.
April 2014 - Present	After results in March's local elections indicating that the AKP retained substantial popular appeal, Parliament passes laws boosting the power of Turkey's intelligence

service and providing for the ultimate closure of private tutoring centers. In June, a court overturns 230 of the Sledgehammer alleged coup convictions on due process grounds, with the defendants to be retried. In July, dozens of police personnel are arrested for allegedly using a terrorist investigation as a pretext to wiretap Erdogan and other top government officials, with many in the media interpreting the arrests as an attempt by the government to weaken the Gulen movement.

Erdogan Government and Gulen Movement: Competing Narratives

Common pro-Erdogan narratives hold that the Gulen movement has directly controlled large elements of the criminal justice sector in Turkey for a number of years. Those who accept these narratives often assert that because many of the same prosecutors from the Ergenekon and Sledgehammer cases were involved with the corruption cases against the government, the Gulen movement is behind all of the cases, and that questions from the former cases regarding whether political motivations led to evidentiary/due process infractions or irregularities also apply to the latter. Many also claim that the corruption cases were timed to hurt the AKP in upcoming elections through voter disaffection and loss of investor confidence. Leaks of audio recordings that are claimed to reveal compromising information about Erdogan and other high-level AKP officials have led purveyors of pro-Erdogan narratives to allege that the Gulen movement maintains an extensive intelligence and surveillance operation, feeding existing conspiracy theories about possible Gulen movement collaboration with foreign countries.

Common narratives from Gulen movement adherents and sympathizers or those defending the initial prosecutorial team that brought the December 2013 corruption charges hold that evidence linking Turkish civil servants with the movement is purely conjectural. Such narratives also claim that Erdogan and his inner circle are resorting to illegal profiling methods and broad generalizations to target a wide swath of loyal state employees. According to these narratives, this is part of an effort to create a fictitious bogeyman to maximize short-term electoral advantages and distract Turkey's citizens from Erdogan's alleged corruption and purported efforts to more fully consolidate his personal power. These pro-Gulen movement/initial prosecutorial team narratives often claim that the timing of the corruption-related arrests was incidental to political events, and took place as soon as possible after a careful gathering of evidence. Perhaps reflecting the Gulen movement's international presence and influence, arguments by Gulen and his adherents and sympathizers often appear to be crafted to elicit international support—often in international fora and media outlets, such as Gulen's January 2014 interviews with the *Wall Street Journal* and the BBC[62]—and in reference to universal standards of democratic governance and human rights (such as the criteria for European Union accession).

Third-party observers have taken a range of positions on recent domestic developments in Turkey. Some criticize both Erdogan and the Gulen movement for the current situation in varying ways and to varying degrees. Some opine or imply that because Turkey's constitutional system may not be optimally designed to enforce checks and balances, and because formal opposition parties to the AKP are presumably relatively weak, the counterpoise between Erdogan and the Gulen movement may strengthen Turkey's democracy.[63]

Some Erdogan colleagues and pro-government media have explicitly or implicitly accused the United States and other international actors (such as Israel, the Jewish diaspora, and various multinational companies and media outlets) of conspiring with or otherwise facilitating the Gulen movement's alleged efforts to undermine or even overthrow Erdogan. Such speculation is intertwined with increased scrutiny in Turkish media of some observers' claims regarding Gulen movement ties with the United States. This is fueled to some extent by Gulen's move to Pennsylvania in the late 1990s (ostensibly for health reasons) while facing charges of

---

[62] Joe Parkinson and Jay Solomon, op. cit.; "Turkey's Fethullah Gulen denies corruption probe links," *BBC News*, January 27, 2014.

[63] See, e.g., Akyol, "More Divisions, More Democracy," op. cit.

undermining secularism in Turkey, and his receipt of U.S. permanent residency status in 2008. After pro-government media insinuated in December 2013 that Francis Ricciardone, then U.S. ambassador to Turkey, had made statements potentially undermining the government, and Erdogan obliquely denounced "provocative actions" by ambassadors, Ricciardone portrayed the accusations as false and demanded that they cease.[64] Since then, they largely have. Erdogan has publicly expressed his interest in having the Obama Administration deport or extradite Fethullah Gulen, though most observers assert that the Administration is unlikely to do this. A Turkish journalist has written that Erdogan appears to be "playing more to his domestic gallery by creating the impression that he is pressuring the United States."[65]

In an apparent effort to increase his government's control over the criminal justice sector and probably to marginalize purported Gulen movement adherents and sympathizers, Erdogan has made massive personnel changes among prosecutors and police. He has reportedly reassigned thousands of police (largely from Istanbul and Ankara) to other parts of the country. In February 2014, he championed parliamentary legislation that established justice ministry control over the country's Supreme Board of Judges and Prosecutors (HSYK). This law will most likely prevent future criminal investigations from taking place without the approval of Erdogan-appointed politicians.[66]

Following these changes, no additional arrests have been made in relation to the corruption investigations, and those who were charged in December 2013 have been released on parole awaiting trial. Some prosecutors involved in initiating the investigations, who have since been reassigned, have alleged that the government is refusing to prosecute additional cases. Additionally, several documents and audio recordings apparently reinforcing corruption-related allegations have been anonymously leaked to media outlets and on social media Internet sites. These leaks include phone calls purported to be between Erdogan and his son Bilal (Erdogan vigorously denies the calls' authenticity) discussing the transfer of large sums of money to avoid detection. This has prompted Erdogan and his government and AKP colleagues to allege the existence of a vast Gulen movement-controlled operation to monitor their communications, possibly with outside help—reinforcing conspiracy theories regarding U.S. or other international involvement. The crucial role of the Internet in circulating leaked information portraying Erdogan and his government in a negative light probably largely motivated the Turkish parliament's passage of a February 2014 law allowing the government wider authority to block websites, and the government's spring 2014 bans on Twitter and YouTube that were eventually overturned by Turkey's constitutional court.

---

[64] Semih Idiz, "US-Turkey crisis averted over corruption probe," *Al-Monitor Turkey Pulse*, December 24, 2013.

[65] Semih Idiz, "Does Erdogan really want Gulen in Turkey?," *Al-Monitor Turkey Pulse*, May 6, 2014.

[66] Previous to the February 2014 HSYK law, a 2010 popular referendum to amend Turkey's constitution had included a provision reportedly intended to keep the justice minister as chair of the HSYK, while preserving the judiciary's independence by preventing the justice minister from active participation in its work. *The Silent Revolution: Turkey's Democratic Change and Transformation Inventory: 2002-2012*, Republic of Turkey, Prime Ministry, Undersecretariat of Public Order and Security, October 2013, p. 96. Turkey's Constitutional Court is considering the validity of the February 2014 law.

Broader Concerns Regarding Rule of Law, Civil Liberties, and Secular Governance[67]

Some observers argue that events since the nationwide June 2013 protests have led to increasingly authoritarian governance by Erdogan. For example, a February 2014 Freedom House report purported to connect recent events with supposedly already established patterns of behavior involving widespread intimidation and manipulation of media, private companies, and other civil society actors through a number of means, including active interference in their operations and regulatory action to compel government-friendly outcomes.[71] One Turkish

---

Corruption Allegations and Iran- and Al Qaeda-Related Claims[68]

Alleged evidence connected with the December 2013 corruption-related arrests has been leaked to various media sources. In addition to evidence that a number of Turkish businessmen engaged in "tender-rigging," or paying bribes to public officials in exchange for preferential treatment of their bids for public contracts and zoning exceptions, some of the most high-profile charges revolve around an apparent arrangement by Turkish cabinet ministers to engage in "gold-for-energy" trades with Iranian sources between March 2012 (when international money transfers to Iran through the SWIFT system were prohibited) and July 2013 (when energy transactions with Iran using precious metals became subject to U.S. sanctions). See "Iran" for more information.

Media reports citing leaked case files or evidence suggest that an Iranian native and recently-naturalized Turkish citizen named Riza Sarraf (formerly Reza Zarrab) headed a courier operation by which billions of dollars' worth of gold was apparently exported to Iran—sometimes directly, sometimes through Dubai. Sarraf apparently paid millions of dollars of bribes to then Turkish Economy Minister Zafer Caglayan and then Halkbank (a publicly-owned Turkish bank) general manager Suleyman Aslan. Media accounts of the December 2013 arrests stated that $4.5 million dollars were found in shoeboxes in Aslan's home. Caglayan reportedly favored the gold-shipping arrangement in part because it boosted Turkey's export figures.

Leaks also allege that Saudi national Yasin al Qadi entered Turkey privately four times between February and October 2012 with the assistance of Turkish government security. Until October 5, 2012, al Qadi was subject to a United Nations Security Council-imposed travel ban and asset freeze because of allegations that he had helped finance activities of Al Qaeda. The U.S. Treasury Department continues to list al Qadi as a Specially Designated Global Terrorist.[69] The recent revelations claim that one of the purposes of al Qadi's business in Turkey was involvement in a possible sale of public land below market value, and that he met personally with Prime Minister Erdogan's son Bilal. In 2006, Prime Minister Erdogan said that he knew al Qadi and that it was "impossible" for al Qadi to associate with or support a terrorist organization. A 2008 *Forbes* article had previously raised questions about possible al Qadi dealings in Turkey.[70]

---

[67] For additional information, see the State Department's 2013 Country Report on Human Rights for Turkey.

[68] Sources for the Iran-related material in this textbox include Mehul Srivastava, "Turkey Crisis Puts Jailed Millionaire at Heart of Gold-Smuggling Ring," *Bloomberg*, January 29, 2014; Fehim Tastekin (translated from Turkish), "Iranian gold stars in Turkish corruption scandal," *Al-Monitor Turkey Pulse*, December 20, 2013; Jonathan Schanzer and Mark Dubowitz, "Iran's Turkish gold rush," *Sunday's Zaman*, December 27, 2013. Sources for the Al Qaeda-related material include United Nations Press Release, "Security Council Committee Concerning Afghanistan Issues a Further Addendum," SC/7180, October 19, 2001; United Nations Press Release, "Al-Qaida Sanctions Committee Deletes Entry of Yasin Abdullah Ezzedine Qadi from Its List," SC/10785, October 5, 2012; Ali Aslan Kilic, "Yasin al-Qadi escorted by PM's security detail, daily reports," *Today's Zaman*, December 30, 2013; Samuel Rubenfeld, "UN Removes Saudi Businessman from Al Qaeda Blacklist," wsj.com, October 8, 2012; Richard C. Morais with Denet C. Tezel, "The Al-Qadi Affair," *Forbes*, January 24, 2008.

[69] Al Qadi has also been listed on and de-listed from terrorism-related blacklists in the European Union, Switzerland, and the United Kingdom.

[70] Morais, op. cit.

[71] Freedom House, *Democracy in Crisis: Corruption, Media, and Power in Turkey*, February 2014.

---

journalist has commented:

> All this has confirmed that, after a dozen years in power, the system Mr. Erdogan established is a textbook case of illiberal democracy—a system whereby the ruler comes to power through elections but is not bound by the rule of law and shows little respect for civil liberties. It is much more similar to Vladimir V. Putin's Russia than the liberal democracies of Western Europe that Turkey hopes to emulate.[72]

Even before the June 2013 protests, domestic and international observers had raised concerns about Erdogan's and the AKP government's level of respect for civil liberties.[73] Although infringement upon press freedom has long been a concern in Turkey, measures taken by authorities in recent years have been widely criticized as unusually severe and ideologically driven. These measures include various means of criminal prosecution or reported intimidation, often under a law on terrorism that many human rights organizations and international observers criticize for being vague and overly broad. A May 2014 mining disaster in the western city of Soma, which resulted in 301 fatalities, raised additional questions in the media regarding the Turkish government's competence and responsiveness to citizens' concerns.

Given the weakening of the military within the political system, some Turks have expressed uncertainty about the extent to which checks and balances in Turkey's government protect secular or nonreligious civic participation and lifestyles from Erdogan's charismatic and Islamic-friendly single-party rule.[74] Since the AKP came to power, the military has reportedly become less scrutinizing of its rising officers' religious backgrounds and views; regulations on the consumption of alcohol have increased; Islamic education has been accorded greater prominence within the public school curriculum; and the wearing of headscarves by women in government buildings, universities, and other public places has gained legal and social acceptance. Such developments, among others, prompted this observation in the Albright-Hadley report:

> To ensure social stability and a democratic trajectory, it is thus incumbent on the new establishment to reassure secular-minded Turks that their way of life has a place in Turkish society, even if secularists failed to do the same for observant Muslims during their long period of ascendancy.[75]

Erdogan and his close advisors have distanced themselves from the Ergenekon and Sledgehammer (*Balyoz*) cases against the military that they formerly backed, now portraying them as primarily Gulen movement-influenced prosecutions. This has led some observers to

---

[72] Mustafa Akyol, "McCarthyism Comes to Turkey," *New York Times*, March 20, 2014.

[73] Council on Foreign Relations, op. cit., p. 23: "In some areas, the AKP-led government has used the same nondemocratic tools as its predecessor, making it appear no more liberal than previous Turkish governments." According to Reporters Without Borders's 2013 World Press Freedom Index, Turkey is the 154th "freest" country out of 179 evaluated, down six places from 2012. The Committee to Protect Journalists reported in December 2013 that Turkey was the world's leading jailer of journalists for the second consecutive year (though the number reported declined from 49 in 2012 to 40 in 2013), closely followed by Iran and China. Freedom House's *Freedom of the Press* report for 2014, released in May, listed Turkey's media environment as "not free" (changed from the previous year's designation of "partly free"). Karin Deutsch Karlekar, "Why Is Turkey's Media Environment Ranked 'Not Free'?," Freedom House, May 12, 2014.

[74] For example, Erdogan's statements in November 2013 criticizing co-ed housing arrangements among university students has triggered heated public debate about the extent to which public officials should involve themselves in conduct that many Turks regard as private. See, e.g., Sinan Ülgen, "Turkey needs more liberalism with its democracy," *Financial Times*, December 3, 2013.

[75] Council on Foreign Relations, op. cit., p. 17.

speculate that Erdogan's actions could open the door for the military to eventually regain a place in Turkey's political sphere.[76] In early 2014, the government abolished the special courts that had heard the military cases, and in June 2014, Turkey's highest criminal court ordered the release and retrial of 230 military officers who had been convicted in the Sledgehammer case in 2012.[77]

Domestic Political and Economic Implications: 2014-2015 Elections and Erdogan's Future

With Turkish presidential and parliamentary elections scheduled for August 2014 and June 2015, respectively, recent controversies and broader concerns influence domestic questions regarding power, constitutional democracy, civil liberties, economic stability and growth, as well as Turkey's regional and global profile. It remains unclear how these developments will ultimately impact Prime Minister Erdogan's hold on the government and overall legacy, and Turkey's relations with the United States. Since the nationwide protests in June 2013, protests have periodically recurred on a smaller scale, leading to speculation over the possibility of larger demonstrations in the event of polarizing outcomes or suspected voting irregularities in coming elections.[78]

On July 1, 2014, Erdogan announced his candidacy in Turkey's first-ever direct presidential election, scheduled for August 2014. Most media sources expect Erdogan to win, especially following local elections in March 2014 indicating that the AKP retained substantial popular appeal.[79] According to one U.S.-based analyst, "Erdogan's electoral strategy envisions strong support among European Turks [who will be able to vote outside of Turkey for the first time] in the first round of voting, and backing from nationalist Kurds in case of a second round. Together, the Turks in Europe and the Kurds could help Erdogan win the 50% of the vote needed to become president."[80] Parliamentary elections are scheduled to take place no later than June 2015.

Much debate focuses on the possibility that Erdogan, if he wins the August 2014 election, might seek to expand and consolidate power in the presidency and maintain control over the AKP and

---

[76] See, e.g., Omer Taspinar, "An Egyptian Model for Turkey?," *todayszaman.com*, January 12, 2014; Orhan Kemal Cengiz (translated from Turkish), "Will Turkish corruption scandal lead to return of military to politics?," *Al-Monitor Turkey Pulse*, January 12, 2014.

[77] The court's decision to overturn the convictions was based on due process concerns that had been raised throughout and after the initial trial. Some media commentators implied that the judicial reversal might be connected with Erdogan's public differences with the Gulen movement. Ceylan Yeginsu, "Turkish Officers Convicted in 2012 Coup Case Are Released," *New York Times*, June 19, 2014.

[78] Most recently, the early March 2014 death and funeral of Istanbul teenager Berkin Elvan from a wound he sustained from a tear gas canister during the June 2013 protests sparked demonstrations in Turkish cities that led to the death of a young man in Istanbul and a police officer in Tunceli.

[79] In June 2014, the two main opposition parties, the Republican People's Party (CHP) and the Nationalist Action Party (MHP), nominated former diplomat and former Organization of Islamic Cooperation Secretary General Ekmeleddin Ihsanoglu as their joint presidential candidate. In July, the Kurdish nationalist Peoples' Democratic Party (HDP), many of whose members previously belonged to the Peace and Democracy Party (BDP), nominated one of its two co-chairs, Selahattin Demirtas, as its candidate.

[80] Soner Cagaptay, with Ege Cansu Sacikara, "Turks in Europe and Kurds in Turkey Could Elect Erdogan," Washington Institute for Near East Policy, PolicyWatch #2291, July 23, 2014.

---

his prime ministerial successor, either formally or informally. For this reason, many observers view the upcoming elections as particularly consequential.[81]

Despite criticism inside and outside of Turkey saying that Erdogan shows insufficient regard for minority rights and views, his government has initiated a peace process with the Kurdistan Workers' Party (PKK),[82] a political group and militia seeking greater rights for Turkey's approximately 15 million ethnic Kurdish citizens. As mentioned above, Erdogan may be counting on Kurdish votes in upcoming elections, but still may be reluctant to make significant changes to Turkey's political system and society benefitting the Kurds, if at all, until after the elections, given strong residual Turkish nationalist sentiment and concerns about transnational links between Turkey's Kurds and Kurds in Iraq, Syria, and (to a lesser extent) Iran.

Since 2012, Turkey's economy has grown slowly in comparison with recent years. Additionally, since 2013, questions regarding political stability have combined with other structural factors, including global expectations for a tighter U.S. monetary policy and Turkey's sizeable current account deficit, to weaken the Turkish lira considerably. Turkey's central bank aggressively raised interest rates in January 2014, somewhat quieting—if not eliminating—international investor concerns. To date, current financial concerns have not triggered popular panic on the level of past Turkish experiences with bank troubles and inflation. However, given the growth of the Turkish middle class and standards of living since the AKP took power in 2002, it is unclear how current economic realities and expectations might drive voter participation and attitudes. Over two separate occasions in May and June, the central bank has since lowered the benchmark interest rate by 1.25 percentage points from where it was raised in January, but Erdogan continues to advocate for it to cut rates more sharply. This has led some observers to voice concern at Erdogan's apparent attempts at intervention.[83]

U.S. and European Union Approaches

U.S. officials' ability to influence Turkish domestic developments is unclear. Some observers are urging U.S. policymakers to become more publicly vocal in signaling that what they characterize as authoritarian and demagogic behavior in Turkey may endanger the country's democratic institutions and its relations with the United States.[84] Some who express these views have suggested greater emphasis on human rights and democracy concerns alongside the security and economic dimensions of the bilateral strategic relationship.[85] However, other observers counsel that U.S. policymakers use discretion in communicating concerns regarding rule of law, civil liberties, and political and economic stability in Turkey. Two U.S.-based analysts assert that U.S. positions have limited influence on internal Turkish affairs, and assert that experiences in the past

---

[81] Murat Yetkin, "Turkey's future: Strong president or balanced democracy?," *Hurriyet Daily News*, July 7, 2014.

[82] The PKK is designated as a terrorist organization by the United States and the European Union.

[83] "Erdogan's sniping at Central Bank will not help," *Agence France Presse*, July 6, 2014.

[84] Bipartisan Letter to President Obama on Turkey (from 84 U.S. former policymakers and analysts, including two former ambassadors to Turkey and four former Members of Congress), Foreign Policy Initiative, February 20, 2014.

[85] Freedom House, op. cit. This report proposes that the United States pursue free trade agreement negotiations with Turkey in parallel with the Transatlantic Trade and Investment Partnership talks it has initiated with the European Union, and that any final agreement ultimately should be linked to Turkey's transparency and accountability in all business and financial dealings.

50 years have shown that the Turkish people "will bristle at U.S. efforts to 'punish' a given Turkish government for decisions Washington thinks are inadvisable."[86]

The Obama Administration appears to be concerned about current developments in Turkey, but may be reluctant to insert itself into the country's domestic affairs during a crucial election season. This may reflect a concern that going beyond rhetorical support for traditional U.S. values such as limited government and freedom of expression has the potential to entangle them in controversies among various individuals and groups vying for power and political survival or advantage. The White House readout of a February 19, 2014, telephone call between President Obama and Erdogan indicates that the President made reference to "the importance of sound policies rooted in the rule of law to reassure the financial markets, nurture a predictable investment environment, strengthen bilateral ties, and benefit the future of Turkey."[87] Some Members of Congress have proposed resolutions in both the House (H.Res. 532) and Senate (S.Res. 403) calling for greater media freedom, and some have asked President Obama to raise concerns regarding rule of law, checks and balances, and civil liberties with Turkey's leaders.[88] In response to questioning at his July 15, 2014, Senate Foreign Relations European Affairs Subcommittee nomination hearing from Senator John McCain, John Bass, the Administration's ambassador-designate for Turkey, acknowledged that recent actions by Erdogan constituted a "drift" in the direction of authoritarianism.

Strategic cooperation between the United States and Turkey has been complicated by a number of issues discussed in this report, and it is unclear whether cooperation is likely to improve in the event of change or uncertainty regarding Turkey's leadership. Turkey's current U.S.-supported efforts to reach political accommodation with its Kurds, although possibly stemming from regional realities that most potential Turkish leaders would likely address, remain strongly associated by most observers with Erdogan. He has demonstrated a personal willingness to initiate and maintain a negotiating process with Kurdistan Workers' Party (PKK) leader Abdullah Ocalan.

A variety of European leaders and institutions have voiced concern about recent developments in Turkey. These concerns reflect the dilemmas that backsliding on rule of law and civil liberties could pose for Turkey's prospects of membership in or closer relations with the EU (see **Appendix E**). In a March 2014 resolution, the European Parliament made a number of points, including the following:

> [Parliament e]xpresses deep concern at the recent developments in Turkey with regard to allegations of high-level corruption; regrets the removal of the prosecutors and police officers in charge of the original investigations, as this goes against the fundamental principle of an independent judiciary and deeply affects the prospects for credible investigations; considers regrettable the serious breakdown of trust between the government, the judiciary, the police and the media; urges the Government of Turkey, therefore, to show

---

[86] See, e.g., Soner Cagaptay and James F. Jeffrey, "Turkey's 2014 Political Transition: From Erdogan to Erdogan?," op. cit.

[87] Readout available at http://www.whitehouse.gov/the-press-office/2014/02/19/readout-president-obama-s-call-prime-minister-erdogan.

[88] "Members of Congress express concerns over Erdoğan in letter to Obama," *Today's Zaman*, March 30, 2014. See also a letter from Representatives Eliot Engel and William Keating entitled "Relations with Turkey" in the *Economist*, June 14, 2014.

full commitment to democratic principles and to refrain from any further interference in the investigation and prosecution of corruption.[89]

The Kurdish Issue

Ethnic Kurds reportedly constitute approximately 18% of Turkey's population, though a number of differing claims exist. Kurds are largely concentrated in urban areas and the relatively impoverished southeastern region of the country, but pockets exist throughout the country. Kurdish reluctance to recognize Turkish state authority—a dynamic that also exists between Kurds and national governments in Iraq, Iran, and Syria—and harsh Turkish measures to quell Kurdish identity- and rights-based claims and demands have fed tensions that have periodically worsened since the foundation of the republic in 1923. Since 1984, the Turkish military has waged an on-and-off struggle to put down a separatist insurgency and urban terrorism campaign by the PKK (whose founder, Abdullah Ocalan, is profiled in **Appendix A**).[90] The initially secessionist demands of the PKK have since evolved to a less ambitious goal of greater cultural and political autonomy.

The struggle between Turkish authorities and the PKK was most intense during the 1990s, but resumed in 2003 after the U.S.-led invasion of Iraq, following an intervening lull. According to the U.S. government, the PKK partially finances its activities through criminal activities, including its operation of a Europe-wide drug trafficking network.[91] The PKK has used safe havens in northern Iraq to coordinate and launch attacks at various points since the end of the 1991 Gulf War. Amid internal conflict in Syria since 2011, the PKK's Syrian sister organization, the Democratic Union of Syria (PYD), has gained a measure of control over a swath of Kurdish-populated territory near Syria's border with Turkey. This raises questions for Turkey about the possibility of another base of support for PKK training, leadership, and operations.[92]

Turkey's AKP government has acknowledged that the integration of Kurds into Turkish society will require political, cultural, and economic development approaches in addition to the more traditional security-based approach. The Turkish military's approach to neutralizing the PKK has been routinely criticized by Western governments and human rights organizations for being overly hard on ethnic Kurds—thousands have been imprisoned for PKK involvement or sympathies

PKK Designations by U.S. Government	
Designation	Year
Foreign Terrorist Organization	1997
Specially Designated Global Terrorist	2001
Significant Foreign Narcotics Trafficker	2008

---

[89] European Parliament resolution of 12 March 2014 on the 2013 progress report on Turkey (2013/2945(RSP)).

[90] In footnote 2 of a September 2011 report, the International Crisis Group stated that Turkish government figures estimate that 11,700 Turks have been killed since fighting began in the early 1980s. This figure includes Turkish security personnel of various types and Turkish civilians (including Turkish Kurds who are judged not to have been PKK combatants). The same report states that Turkish estimates of PKK dead during the same time period run from 30,000 to 40,000. International Crisis Group, *Turkey: Ending the PKK Insurgency*, Europe Report No. 213, September 20, 2011.

[91] U.S. Treasury Department Press Release, "Five PKK Leaders Designated Narcotics Traffickers," April 20, 2011.

[92] However, northern Syria's more open terrain and comparably small and dispersed Kurdish population may make it a less plausible base of operations than Iraq. Syria hosted the PKK's leadership until 1998, and historical and personal links persist among Syrian Kurds and the PKK.

and hundreds of thousands have been displaced.

The AKP has a sizeable constituency in rural Kurdish areas because of its appeal to traditional values. By appealing to common Islamic identity, Erdogan and other government ministers have moved away from the state's past unwillingness to acknowledge the multiethnic nature of Turkey's citizenry. The government has adopted some measures allowing greater use of Kurdish languages in education, election campaigns, and the media.[93] Nevertheless, past AKP efforts aimed at giving greater rights to Kurds and greater normalized status to Kurdish nationalist leaders and former militants were politically undermined by upswings in violence and public manifestations of nationalist pride among ethnic Turks and ethnic Kurds.[94]

Despite these negative signs, Prime Minister Erdogan publicly revealed in late December 2012 that Turkish intelligence had been conducting negotiations with imprisoned PKK leader Abdullah Ocalan in an attempt to get the PKK to disarm. In late March 2013, Ocalan and other PKK leaders declared a cease-fire, although its durability may depend on the government's ability to persuade the PKK and other Kurds that it sincerely seeks to address the issues of key importance to them. PKK militants who had been withdrawing from Turkey (presumably to northern Iraq) as part of the peace process reportedly stopped doing so in early September 2013.[95] In late September, Erdogan announced a package of domestic reforms that featured measures favoring even greater expression of Kurdish identity and language in Turkish national life, alongside a number of provisions contemplating electoral reform and intending to address some individual liberties and the concerns of other minorities. Kurdish leaders generally acknowledged the reform package as a step in the right direction, but as not going far enough.[96] In June 2014, the Turkish parliament formally adopted Erdogan's peace process approach.

Observers express a range of opinions regarding the advisability and prospects of negotiations, as well as the extent to which Ocalan and the PKK represent Turkey's Kurds. Many observers agree that Erdogan's public acknowledgment of the talks was a bold step that could mobilize broad public support for a deal, but that it also presented a dilemma: "continuing toward peace will anger Turkey's nationalists; but failing to live up to its agreement could lead to a new wave of Kurdish violence."[97] Some commentators theorize that Erdogan authorized the PKK talks in 2012 to bolster his chances for the presidency. Other theories suggested that Erdogan was trying to

---

[93] Kurdish nationalist leaders demand that any future changes to Turkey's 1982 constitution not suppress Kurdish ethnic and linguistic identity. The first clause of Article 3 of the constitution reads, "The Turkish state, with its territory and nation, is an indivisible entity. Its language is Turkish." Because the constitution states that its first three articles are unamendable, even proposing a change could face judicial obstacles. Kurds in Turkey also seek to modify the electoral law to allow for greater Kurdish nationalist participation in Turkish politics by lowering the percentage-vote threshold (currently 10%) for political parties in parliament. In the 2011 election, 61 members of the Kurdish nationalist Peace and Democracy Party (BDP) or affiliated independents ran as independents for individual geographic constituencies because of a calculation that the party would not reach the 10% threshold. In the aggregate, these independents won 6% of the national vote.

[94] The International Crisis Group stated that the time period from the summer of 2011 until March 2013 featured the worst fighting between the PKK and Turkish authorities since the 1990s, reporting that at least 928 people had been killed in that time—"at least 304 security forces, police and village guards, 533 militants and 91 civilians." International Crisis Group, *Crying "Wolf": Why Turkish Fears Need Not Block Kurdish Reform,* Europe Report No. 227, October 7, 2013.

[95] Piotr Zalewski, "Turkey's Imperfect Peace," *foreignaffairs.com,* October 20, 2013.

[96] See, e.g., Ilter Turan, "Democratization from Above: Erdoğan's Democracy Package," *On Turkey,* German Marshall Fund of the United States, October 22, 2013.

[97] Bipartisan Policy Center, op. cit., p. 8.

---

defuse potential PKK threats from Syria or to take advantage of intra-Kurdish divisions and Ocalan's personal desire for freedom. In a February 2013 interview with a Turkish journalist, President Obama was quoted as saying, "I applaud Prime Minister Erdogan's efforts to seek a peaceful resolution to a struggle that has caused so much pain and sorrow for the people of Turkey for more than 30 years."[98]

Economy

Overview of Macroeconomic Factors and Trade

The AKP's political successes have been aided considerably by robust Turkish economic growth that was set back only briefly as a result of the 2008-2009 global economic crisis. Growth rates, fueled by diversified Turkish conglomerates (such as Koc and Sabanci) from traditional urban centers as well as "Anatolian tigers" (small- to medium-sized, export-oriented businesses concentrated in central and southern Turkey), were comparable in the past decade to those of China, India, and other major developing economies. A March 2014 analysis stated that Turkey's citizens are 43% better off economically now than when Erdogan became prime minister.[99]

The dependence of Turkey's economy—saddled with a relatively high current account deficit—on foreign capital and exports has led to challenges stemming from the economic slowdown in the European Union, Turkey's main trading partner. According to the Turkish Statistical Institute, growth slowed from 8.8% in 2011 to 2.1% in 2012, but rebounded to 4.0% in 2013.[100] The Turkish central bank's decision to aggressively raise interest rates in January 2014 to strengthen its falling currency (discussed above) has set back growth expectations for 2014, from initial forecasts near 4% to closer to 2-3%.[101] As major elections are held in coming months, questions of political stability could influence economic activity and foreign investment. Some analysts have also raised concerns about companies in the Turkish private sector with significant short-term debt who may face difficulty refinancing given recently-raised rates and dependence on external funding flows.

Some analyses of Turkey's economy assert that the "low-hanging fruit"—numerous large infrastructure projects and the scaling up of low-technology manufacturing—that largely drove the previous decade's economic success following a major 2000-2001 domestic financial crisis, in tandem with International Monetary Fund-guided reforms, is unlikely to produce similar results going forward.[102] Structural economic goals for Turkey include incentivizing greater research and development to encourage Turkish technological innovation and global competitiveness, harmonizing the educational system with future workforce needs, encouraging domestic savings, and increasing and diversifying energy supplies to meet ever-growing consumption demands.

---

[98] Interview of President Barack Obama by Pinar Ersoy of *Milliyet*, quoted in "Obama 'applauds' Turkey's effort to find peaceful solution to Kurdish problem," *hurriyetdailynews.com*, February 10, 2013.

[99] Christopher de Bellaigue, "Turkey Goes Out of Control," *New York Review of Books*, April 3, 2014 Issue (accessed online on March 25, 2014).

[100] Turkish Statistical Institute, *Turkey in Statistics 2013*, p. 78. Economist Intelligence Unit, *Country Report: Turkey*, generated March 25, 2014.

[101] de Bellaigue, op. cit.; International Monetary Fund 2014 World Outlook Database, accessed August 1, 2014; Economist Intelligence Unit, *Country Report: Turkey*, generated July 29, 2014.

[102] See, e.g., Daniel Dombey, "Six Markets to Watch: Turkey," *Foreign Affairs*, January/February 2014.

Through monetary and fiscal policy and various regulatory practices, Turkish policymakers may seek to attract more equity and foreign direct investment inflows and fewer short-term loans and portfolio inflows. The former generally are accompanied by skill and technology transfers, while the latter are more prone to sudden reversal.[103]

The European Union is Turkey's main trading partner by far, while the United States is Turkey's fourth-largest trading partner (behind the EU, Russia, and China). Turkey is the United States's 34th-largest trading partner.[104] Though Turkish pursuit of new markets since 1992 has reduced trade with the EU (from nearly 50% to less than 40%) and with the United States (from 9% to around 5%) as a percentage of Turkey's total trade, overall trade volume with both is generally trending upward.[105]

Table 2. U.S. Merchandise Trade with Turkey

($ in millions)

	2007	2008	2009	2010	2011	2012	2013
Exports	6,500	9,960	7,090	10,550	14,660	12,580	12,070
Imports	4,600	4,640	3,660	4,200	5,220	6,230	6,670
Total Volume	11,100	14,600	10,750	14,750	19,880	18,810	18,740

Source: U.S. Department of Commerce, Foreign Trade Division, U.S. Census Bureau.

Despite concerns by U.S. senior business executives regarding Turkey's legal and regulatory system and other issues according to a 2011 survey, 65% of these businesspeople indicated willingness to invest further in Turkey. Additionally, 88% advocated more U.S. government engagement with Turkey's government to "improve the investment, market access, and operating climate for US companies in Turkey."[106]

Energy Issues[107]

Turkey's importance as a regional energy transport hub elevates its increasing relevance for world energy markets while also providing Turkey with opportunities to satisfy its own growing domestic energy needs.[108] Turkey's location has made it a key country in the U.S. and European effort to establish a southern corridor for natural gas transit from diverse sources.[109] However, as

---

[103] See, e.g., *Organisation for Economic Co-operation and Development Surveys: Turkey*, July 2012.

[104] Statistics on Turkey's status relative to other U.S. trading partners compiled by U.S. International Trade Commission, available at http://dataweb.usitc.gov/SCRIPTS/cy_m3_run.asp.

[105] Turkish Statistical Institute, cited in Kemal Kirisci, *Turkey and the Transatlantic Trade and Investment Partnership: Boosting the Model Partnership with the United States*, Brookings Center on the United States and Europe, Turkey Project Policy Paper Number 2, September 2013.

[106] American Business Forum in Turkey, *Business and Investment Climate in Turkey 2011*, October 2011.

[107] Michael Ratner, Specialist in Energy Policy, contributed to this subsection. See "Israel" and **Appendix E** for references to the possible relevance to Turkey of offshore natural gas finds by Israel and the Republic of Cyprus.

[108] Transatlantic Academy, *Getting to Zero: Turkey, Its Neighbors, and the West*, June 2010, citing Turkish government statistics.

[109] The U.S. energy strategy in Europe is designed to work together with European nations and the European Union to seek ways to diversify Europe's energy supplies. The focus of U.S. efforts has been on establishing a southern corridor route for Caspian and Middle Eastern natural gas supplies to be shipped to Europe, generally through pipelines (continued...)

---

one analyst writes, "Turkey's ability to effectively play the energy card to further its foreign policy goals is limited by the extent to which the Turkish economy itself is dependent on energy imports, particularly oil and natural gas from Russia and Iran."[110] Since 1991, trade with Russia as a percentage of Turkey's total trade has more than doubled—from 5% to over 11%—largely due to energy imports. Additionally, a subsidiary of Rosatom (Russia's state-run nuclear company) has entered into an agreement to build and operate what would be Turkey's first nuclear power plant[111] in Akkuyu near the Mediterranean port of Mersin, with construction projected to begin in 2016. Iran is also a major source of Turkish energy (see "Iran" below).

However, in late 2011, Turkey and Azerbaijan reached deals for the transit of natural gas to and through Turkey[112] via a proposed Trans-Anatolian Pipeline (TANAP), with gas projected to begin to flow by 2018. The deals have attracted attention as a potentially significant precedent for transporting non-Russian, non-Iranian energy to Europe. On June 28, 2013, the consortium that controls the Azerbaijani gas fields selected to have TANAP connect with a proposed Trans Adriatic Pipeline (TAP) to Italy.[113] The consortium did not rule out subsequently adding a connection with a proposed Nabucco West pipeline to Austria at a later date when more natural gas is developed, but such an eventuality may be less likely in light of the selection of TAP. Turkey has also sought to increase energy imports from Iraq, including through dealings with the Kurdistan Regional Government involving northern Iraqi oil and gas reserves and pipelines that have generated friction with Iraq's central government (see "Iraq" below). Nevertheless, Turkey also agreed in late 2011 to permit Russia's South Stream pipeline to traverse its Black Sea territorial waters to Bulgaria (from which point the pipeline is proposed to extend through the northern Balkans to Italy), reportedly in exchange for discounts to Turkey on purchases of Russian natural gas.[114]

(...continued)

traversing Turkey. See H.Res. 284, "Expressing the sense of the House of Representatives with respect to promoting energy security of European allies through opening up the Southern Gas Corridor." This draft resolution was unanimously approved for forwarding in September 2013 to the House Foreign Affairs Committee by its Subcommittee on Europe, Eurasia, and Emerging Threats. See also, e.g., Tolga Demiryol, "Turkey's energy security and foreign policy," *Turkish Review*, January/February 2012; Transatlantic Academy, op. cit.

[110] Demiryol, op. cit.

[111] In June 2008, the United States and Turkey signed a 15-year "123 Agreement" for peaceful nuclear cooperation in line with international nuclear non-proliferation norms. Turkey is also a signatory to the Nuclear Non-Proliferation Treaty (NPT) and has a safeguards agreement and additional protocol in place with the International Atomic Energy Agency (IAEA). It is an observer to—not a full participant in—the International Framework for Nuclear Energy Cooperation (IFNEC, formerly known as the Global Nuclear Energy Partnership) founded by the United States, Russia, China, France, and Japan in 2007. IFNEC promotes the peaceful use of nuclear energy by helping establish reprocessing centers for nuclear fuel. Turkey is one of the regional countries that analysts routinely mention could decide to pursue its own nuclear weapons program in the event that one or more countries in the region, such as Iran, achieves or declares a nuclear weapons capability. Israel is generally believed by most analysts to have had a nuclear arsenal since the late 1960s, but it maintains a policy of "nuclear opacity" wherein its nuclear weapons status remains officially undeclared. For discussion of Turkey and nuclear weapons, see "Bilateral and NATO Defense Cooperation" and archived CRS Report R41761, *Turkey-U.S. Defense Cooperation: Prospects and Challenges*, by Jim Zanotti.

[112] The terms of Turkish-Azerbaijani agreement specified that 565 billion-700 billion cubic feet (bcf) of natural gas would transit Turkey, of which 210 bcf would be available for Turkey's domestic use.

[113] BP press release, "Shah Deniz targets Italian and Southeastern European gas markets through Trans Adriatic Pipeline," June 28, 2013. For more information, see CRS Report R42405, *Europe's Energy Security: Options and Challenges to Natural Gas Supply Diversification*, coordinated by Michael Ratner.

[114] In light of Russia's unilateral annexation of Ukraine's Crimean Peninsula in March 2014, Russia may be able to re-route South Stream in a way that does not traverse Turkish territorial waters. William J. Broad, "In Taking Crimea, Putin Gains a Sea of Fuel Reserves," *New York Times*, May 17, 2014.

Figure 3. Major Pipelines Traversing Turkey and Possible Nuclear Power Plants

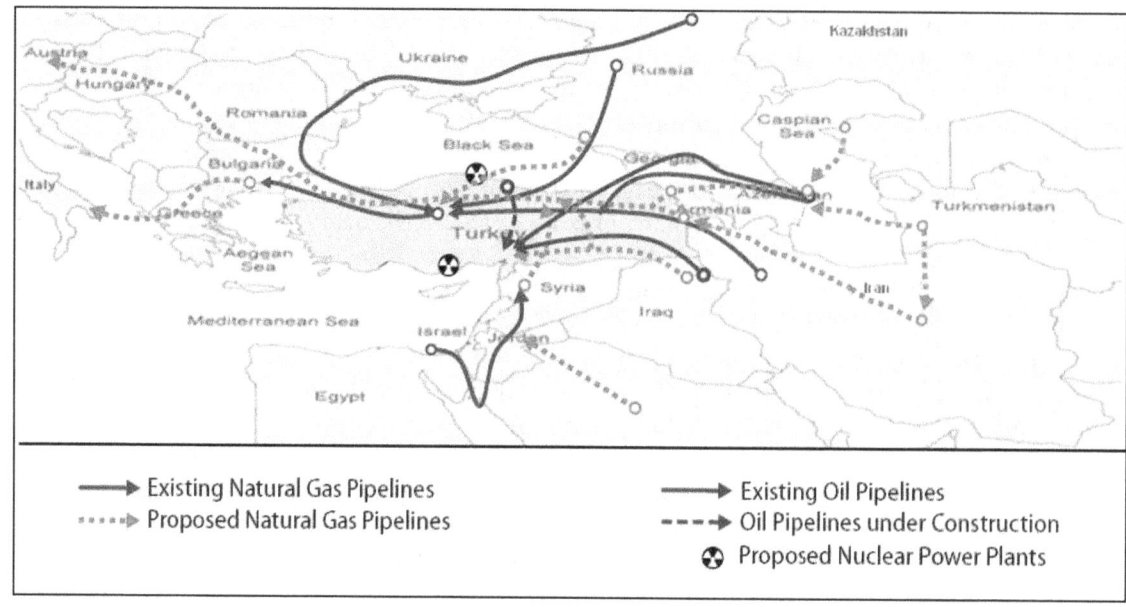

Source: Turkish Economic Ministry, adapted by CRS.

Note: All locations are approximate.

Key Foreign Policy Issues

For information and analysis of foreign policy issues other than the ones below (including European Union, Cyprus, Armenia, and others), see **Appendix E.**

Israel

In the 1990s and early 2000s, Turkey and Israel enjoyed close military ties that fostered cooperation in other areas, including a free trade agreement signed in 2000. In recent years, however, Turkey-Israel relations have worsened. This downturn can be attributed to a number of factors, ranging from Turkish domestic political changes to specific incidents that increased tensions. In terms of change within Turkey, the slide in Turkey-Israel relations reflected the military's declining role in Turkish society, and the greater empowerment of Prime Minister Erdogan and other AKP and national leaders. These leaders seem to view criticism of Israel as both merited and popular domestically and regionally. They often characterize Israeli security measures in the West Bank and especially the Gaza Strip as institutionalized mistreatment of Palestinians. Turkish leaders also have argued that Israel relies too heavily on military capabilities and deterrence (including its undeclared but universally acknowledged nuclear weapons arsenal) in addressing regional problems.

One of the key events that marked the decline in relations was the May 2010 Gaza flotilla incident (mentioned above). Partly to register dissatisfaction with the September 2011 report issued by a U.N. Secretary-General panel of inquiry on the flotilla incident,[115] Turkey

---

[115] The report is available at http://go.ynet.co.il/pic/news/Palmer-Committee-Final-report.pdf. The panel was chaired by (continued...)

downgraded diplomatic relations with Israel to the second secretary level.[116] Turkey's demand for an apology from Israel in connection with the incident was met in March 2013, in a U.S.-facilitated exchange (discussed further below) that was intended to repair the Turkey-Israel rift. Before this, Erdogan prominently registered his disapproval of Israel's military operations in Gaza in December 2008-January 2009, reportedly angry that then Israeli Prime Minister Ehud Olmert did not inform him of Israel's military plans during Olmert's visit to Ankara shortly before the conflict.

Turkey's deteriorated relationship with Israel has presented problems for the United States because of the U.S. desire to coordinate its regional policies with two of its regional allies. U.S. officials seem to have concerns about the repercussions Turkey-Israel tensions could have for regional order and the alignment of U.S. and Turkish interests. This risk could be especially high if Turkey-Israel disagreements on Palestinian issues result in future high-profile incidents. Though Turkey publicly supports a negotiated two-state solution to the Israeli-Palestinian conflict, it backs Palestinian pursuit of United Nations membership and Fatah-Hamas reconciliation, and often criticizes the U.S.-led approach to the peace process. Erdogan also maintains cordial ties with Hamas. In January 2012, he introduced Hamas's prime minister in Gaza, Ismail Haniyeh, as the "elected prime minister of Palestine" at a meeting of AKP parliamentarians in Ankara. During the July 2014 Israel-Gaza conflict, Erdogan has routinely criticized Israel, and Turkey has possibly been involved in international mediation efforts on behalf of Hamas.[117]

Some Members of Congress have shown concern over problematic Turkey-Israel relations.[118] In early 2011, a *New York Times Magazine* article quoted a Turkish diplomat responsible for U.S. relations as saying, "We're getting a lot of flak from the Hill. We used to get hit by the Greek lobby and the Armenian lobby, but we were protected by the Jewish lobby. Now the Jewish lobby is coming after us as well."[119] A U.S.-based analyst who focuses specifically on Israel and Turkey commented in March 2013 that "with the establishment of an Israel-Hellenic caucus in Congress and arms deals with Turkey either being held up or not being introduced into committee at all,

---

(...continued)

former New Zealand Prime Minister Sir Geoffrey Palmer, and included former Colombian President Alvaro Uribe and one participant each from Turkey and Israel. The report expressly provided that its findings were not intended to decide legal questions. Upon the report's leak, Turkish officials disputed the report's finding that Israel's naval blockade of the Gaza Strip was legal, notwithstanding the report's criticism of Israel's handling of the incident itself.

[116] Turkey similarly downgraded diplomatic relations with Israel in 1980 following Israel's enactment of a law on the status of Jerusalem that was deemed a violation of international law by U.N. Security Council Resolution 478. Resolution 478 passed on August 20, 1980 by a vote of 14-0, with the United States as the lone abstention. Turkey reinstated Israel's ambassador in 1992 following the 1991 Madrid Conference that signaled the beginning of the Middle East peace process. Linda Gradstein, "No end in sight for downward spiral in Turkish-Israeli ties," *JTA*, September 6, 2011.

[117] Israeli officials have reportedly leaked to the press the name of a Hamas operational commander living in Turkey who may have links to West Bank-based plots to kidnap Israelis. Matthew Levitt, "Hamas's Not-So-Secret-Weapon," *foreignaffairs.com*, July 9, 2014. Three Israeli teenagers were kidnapped and murdered in June 2014, and this contributed to the outbreak of the July 2014 Israel-Gaza conflict. Hamas denied responsibility for the June 2014 kidnapping.

[118] Following the flotilla incident, the Senate passed S.Res. 548 by voice vote on June 24, 2010. The resolution condemned the attack by the "extremists aboard the Mavi Marmara," invoked Israel's right to self-defense, and encouraged "the Government of Turkey to recognize the importance of continued strong relations with Israel and the necessity of closely scrutinizing organizations with potential ties to terrorist groups" (a reference to the Turkish Islamist non-governmental organization IHH Humanitarian Relief Foundation, the main organizer of the flotilla).

[119] James Traub, "Turkey's Rules," *New York Times Magazine*, January 20, 2011.

---

there is no doubt in my mind that Turkey's feud with Israel is adversely impacting its interests in the U.S."[120]

In March 2013, it appeared that Turkey and Israel might be moving toward some sort of rapprochement. During President Obama's trip to Israel, he and Secretary of State John Kerry facilitated a telephone conversation between Erdogan and Israeli Prime Minister Binyamin Netanyahu.[121] Netanyahu apologized to Erdogan for any operational mistakes by Israel during the flotilla incident "that might have led to the loss of life or injury" and pledged to conclude an agreement on "compensation/nonliability."[122] The apology, on top of other signs that Turkey-Israel relations were slightly improving,[123] led to widespread speculation regarding how much and how fast the two countries' former closeness on military, intelligence, and political matters might be restored.[124] Turkey's energy minister, Taner Yildiz, has publicly contemplated the possibility of Turkish consumption and transport of natural gas from Israel's new offshore discoveries in the Eastern Mediterranean.[125]

However, subsequent developments indicate that substantive rapprochement might be delayed or put off indefinitely. Erdogan's comments (referenced above) holding Israel responsible for the July 2013 military takeover in Egypt and the reports (referenced above) regarding Turkey's alleged disclosure to Iran of the identities of Israeli intelligence sources have complicated the public dimension of efforts to improve Turkey-Israel relations. Turkey's apparent support for Hamas and criticism of Israel during the July 2014 Israel-Gaza conflict may exacerbate these complications. Though there have been indications from Erdogan that Israel-Turkey relations

---

[120] Michael Koplow, "O&Z Goes to Turkey," *ottomansandzionists.com*, March 4, 2013.

[121] U.S. leaders may have felt compelled to broker some sort of improvement in Turkey-Israel relations following remarks Erdogan made in late February 2013 at the United Nations Alliance of Civilizations in Vienna, Austria that appeared to equate Zionism with fascism. Video and partial transcript of remarks and translation available at http://thelede.blogs.nytimes.com/2013/02/28/video-of-turkish-premier-comparing-zionism-to-anti-semitism-and-fascism/?smid=tw-thelede&seid=auto. In a March 12 letter to Erdogan, 89 Members of Congress (including 23 Senators) called on him to retract what they termed his "appalling comment" about Zionism in Vienna, while also stating that they know that Turkey's government "shares a commitment to meaningful international involvement to advance security and peace", and expressing hope for the restoration of good relations between Turkey and Israel. Text of letter available at http://israel house.gov/images/PDF/erdoganletteronzionismcomment.pdf. Erdogan's comparison also drew heavy criticism from Israel, the White House, Secretary Kerry, and some Members of Congress. In a March 19 interview with a prominent Danish news source, although Erdogan did not explicitly retract his Vienna remarks, he was quoted as saying that his criticisms "are directed at Israeli policies" and that "My several statements openly condemning anti-semitism clearly display my position on this issue." "Exclusive Erdogan-interview: 'We see a human tragedy before our eyes,'" *Politiken* (Denmark), March 19, 2013.

[122] Summary of conversation between Netanyahu and Erdogan from Israeli Prime Minister's Office website, March 22, 2013. Turkish officials indicated in the spring of 2014 that they might interpret Israel's allowance of Turkish humanitarian aid shipments to Gaza as a lifting of the closure regime, which is another condition that Erdogan had set forth for the normalization of Turkey-Israel relations.

[123] In December 2012, reports cited a Turkish official as saying that Turkey had withdrawn previous objections to Israel's non-military participation in NATO activities. Gulsen Solaker and Jonathon Burch, "Turkey lifts objection to NATO cooperation with Israel," *Reuters*, December 24, 2012. Israel is part of NATO's Mediterranean Dialogue, along with Algeria, Egypt, Jordan, Morocco, Mauritania, and Tunisia. In addition, trade between the Turkey and Israel has remained on an upward trajectory since the flotilla incident, and by February 2013, Israel had reportedly unblocked the delivery of electronic support measures systems—pursuant to a pre-existing contract—for early warning aircraft that Turkey is purchasing from U.S.-based Boeing. Burak Bekdil, "Israel abandons block on sales to Turkish AWACS," *Hurriyet Daily News*, February 22, 2013.

[124] See, e.g., Oded Eran, "Israel-Turkey Reconciliation Still Remote," *nationalinterest.org*, April 18, 2013.

[125] Amiram Barkat, "Turkish minister: We're interested in Israeli gas," *Globes*, October 31, 2013.

---

could be normalized some time in 2014,[126] debate persists on the extent to which rapprochement is likely, and how it might take place.

Syria[127]

Prime Minister Erdogan and Foreign Minister Davutoglu initially tried to use their then-good relations with Syrian President Bashar al Asad to help broker a peaceful end to the budding Syrian insurgency in 2011. When that failed to moderate Asad's approach to the opposition, they changed tack and adopted a strong stance against the Syrian regime. According to one Turkish journalist:

> In the summer of 2011, Turkey decided to bring down the Baath regime in Damascus and sought ways to implement its decision as much as its capacity allowed. Turkey did everything it could with the exception of direct military intervention in Syria. It is not a secret that Turkey sponsored the initial organization and coordination of the Syrian opposition, opened its territory to the use of the opposition military forces and provided logistical support to them.[128]

In the two years that followed, Turkey coordinated its efforts closely with other countries—including the United States, other NATO allies, and Arab countries such as Saudi Arabia and Qatar—that also provide political, financial, and/or material support to the opposition. It outspokenly advocated for U.N.-backed intervention and—reportedly—has helped funnel assistance to armed Syrian rebel groups, possibly including Al Qaeda-linked Jabhat al Nusra, a U.S.-government designated terrorist organization.[129] As the conflict appeared to exacerbate the longstanding regional Sunni-Shia rivalry between Arab Gulf states supporting the opposition and Iran, which backs the Asad regime, some observers began associating Turkey with these tensions.

Absent a clear endgame in Syria, Turkey focused increasingly on minimizing spillover effects. After some cross-border artillery exchanges in late 2012, Turkey convened consultations with its NATO allies under Article 4 of the North Atlantic Treaty.[130] Although most NATO member states appeared to oppose military intervention in Syria, allied leaders gave approval in December 2012 for the deployment of six Patriot missile batteries to areas near Turkey's southeastern border with Syria.[131]

NATO's Patriot deployment presumably defends against potential Syrian Scud missile and/or chemical weapons attacks, as Turkey does not have a missile defense capability of its own.[132] In

---

[126] Donzis, op. cit.

[127] For background information on Syria, see CRS Report RL33487, *Armed Conflict in Syria: Overview and U.S. Response*, coordinated by Christopher M. Blanchard; and CRS Report R43119, *Syria: Overview of the Humanitarian Response*, by Rhoda Margesson and Susan G. Chesser. Rhoda Margesson, Specialist in International Humanitarian Policy, contributed to the portions of this section on Syrian refugees.

[128] Kadri Gursel, "NATO Patriot Missiles Show Turkey's Military Weakness," *Al-Monitor Turkey Pulse*, December 28, 2012.

[129] Bipartisan Policy Center, op. cit., p. 37. Turkey reportedly denies having assisted extremist organizations in Syria. Ibid., p. 11.

[130] Article 4 reads: "The Parties will consult together whenever, in the opinion of any of them, the territorial integrity, political independence or security of any of the Parties is threatened."

[131] NATO countries also deployed Patriots to Turkey prior to the 1991 and 2003 wars in Iraq.

[132] Turkey's is seeking to address its lack of an independent missile defense capability through the possible deal for T- (continued...)

---

addition to the two batteries and operational teams contributed by the United States to a Turkish military base overlooking the city of Gaziantep, Germany and the Netherlands have each contributed two Patriot batteries and operational teams to bases near the population centers of Karamanmaras and Adana, respectively. The batteries reportedly became operational, under NATO command and control, in late January and early February 2013.[133] Cross-border fire has generally decreased since then. However, potential infiltration of Turkey by militants remains of concern in light of occasional attacks inside Turkey—including in front of the U.S. embassy in Ankara on February 1, 2013.[134] NATO and allied leaders have asserted that the Patriot batteries are deployed for defensive purposes only.[135]

As referenced above, possible Turkish expectations of imminent U.S.-led military action in Syria appear to have dissipated with President Obama's acceptance in September 2013 of a U.N. Security Council-backed agreement regarding chemical weapons removal.[136] Turkey continues to politically engage key regional and international stakeholders in hopes of influencing outcomes in its favor. Turkey also appears to be attentively assessing developments in northern Syria involving the Kurdish PYD (the Syrian sister organization of the PKK), which seems to have obtained a degree of territorial autonomy, and jihadist groups—particularly the Islamic State (also known as ISIL).[137] Some reports indicate that, in response to concerns from the United States in particular, Turkey is more actively seeking to monitor, limit, or deny the use of its territory by Syrian oppositionists affiliated with jihadist movements.[138] In his July 15, 2014, nomination hearing, U.S. ambassador-designate for Turkey John Bass said:

> we've had very good cooperation in recent months in addressing some of the consequences of the conflict in Syria and the increase in fighters' money exploiting Turkey's geography in and out of those conflict zones. Our belief is that the Turks understand this is an acute threat

---

(...continued)

LORAMIDS with Chinese government-owned CPMIEC, as discussed earlier in this report.

[133] NATO press release, "All NATO Patriot batteries in Turkey operational," February 16, 2013.

[134] The Revolutionary People's Liberation Party/Front (DHKP/C, sometimes known as "Dev Sol") claimed responsibility for the embassy bombing, which killed a Turkish security guard. The DHKP/C is a U.S.-designated Foreign Terrorist Organization with a Marxist-Leninist ideology, a long track record of anti-U.S. and anti-NATO militancy, and some historical links with the Asad regime.

[135] On April 11, 2013, Air Force General Philip Breedlove addressed the potential for other uses of NATO's Patriot missile presence in a Senate Armed Services Committee hearing regarding his possible confirmation as U.S. European Command Commander and Supreme Allied Commander, Europe (he was eventually confirmed by the Senate on April 20). In his testimony, General Breedlove stated that the two batteries representing the U.S. contribution "could be used in a role to project into Syria. They have the capability to do it.... if Turkey and the U.S. were looking to do this in a bilateral fashion, or if we could convince our NATO partners to come alongside of us, to also be a part of that."

[136] For more information on Turkey's stance on possible U.S.-led intervention following alleged use of chemical weapons in August 2013 by the Asad regime in an outlying Damascus neighborhood, see CRS Report R43201, *Possible U.S. Intervention in Syria: Issues for Congress*, coordinated by Christopher M. Blanchard and Jeremy M. Sharp.

[137] Some reports had alleged that Turkish officials were lending support to "jihadist fighters" in campaigns against the PYD, but that by late 2013, Turkey may have reduced or ended this alleged support. PYD leader Salih Muslim was quoted as saying that Turkey may have reversed its policy "because of international pressure but also because these groups pose a grave threat to Turkey itself." Amberin Zaman, "Syrian Kurdish leader: Turkey may end proxy war," *Al-Monitor Turkey Pulse*, November 7, 2013.

[138] Dorian Jones, "Turkey Deports Jihadists Linked to Syria Fighting," *Voice of America*, December 3, 2013.

---

for all of us and we've seen some important steps from them to address some of the issues that were potentially making their geography more attractive.[139]

However, some reports suggest that foreign fighters may continue to use Turkish territory for transit to Syria,[140] and that hundreds of Turkish nationals had joined armed Syrian opposition groups.[141] In March 2014, some media reports claimed that Turkish personnel may have either supported or permitted Syrian oppositionists (including jihadists) to use Turkish territory to capture the largely ethnic Armenian town of Kassab, Syria, just over the border near the Mediterranean coast.[142] Turkey denied any role. The Syrian military recaptured the town in June.

Syrian refugees present an ongoing and difficult dilemma for Turkey. According to the United Nations High Commissioner for Refugees (UNHCR), as of July 25, 2014, the Turkish government is operating 22 government-run refugee camps. Refugees are residing in the camps and in urban areas outside the camps. The total number of refugees in Syria who are registered or awaiting registration is now estimated by UNHCR to be close to 808,600 and is projected to increase.[143] The Regional Response Plan, one of two U.N. appeals focused on the Syrian humanitarian crisis, seeks donor contributions to meet protection and assistance needs of Syrian refugees in Turkey.[144] Registration of refugees and camp management are coordinated by the Turkish government's Disaster Relief Agency (AFAD), with operational support from the Turkish Red Crescent and other organizations. UNHCR provides technical advice and assistance.

Various reports reflect a widely held assessment among observers that Turkey has managed so far to avoid systemic threats to its economic well-being from the refugee flows,[145] but it has reportedly shouldered a total cost of more than $2.5 billion,[146] with only a small percentage of that covered by international assistance. Over the past year, social and political costs have reportedly emerged—especially tensions between Sunni refugees and Turkish citizens of Arab Alawite descent in the border province of Hatay.[147] Turks increasingly appear to acknowledge that as the conflict continues, refugees may remain for several years, probably requiring policies for their employment and education. Already, refugees are affecting prices and wages in Turkish

---

[139] Transcript of hearing testimony from Senate Foreign Relations European Affairs Subcommittee, July 15, 2014.

[140] See, e.g., Murat Yetkin, "Syria's foreign fighters in Turkey's target, too," *hurriyetdailynews.com*, June 7, 2014; Transcript of interview with Thomas Hegghammer of the Norwegian Defence Research Establishment on Syria Deeply blog, Karen Leigh, "Q+A: On Foreign Fighters Flowing into Syria," December 2, 2013. In the interview, Hegghammer, who researches militant Islamism with a focus on transnational jihadi groups, said that Turkey "is the main passageway for fighters from the West, and from the rest of the region."

[141] Constanze Letsch, "The sons feared lost to al-Qaida in Syria," *theguardian.com*, November 11, 2013.

[142] Fehim Tastekin, "Fall of Kassab will be costly for Turkey," *Al-Monitor* (originally published in Turkish in *Radikal*), March 31, 2014.

[143] The Turkish government estimates that there are approximately 1,000,000 Syrians in Turkey, when those not registered or soon-to-be registered as refugees are counted. UNHCR Turkey Syrian Refugee Daily Sitrep, July 25, 2014.

[144] United Nations, *2014 Syria Regional Response Plan*.

[145] International Crisis Group, *Blurring the Borders: Syrian Spillover Risks for Turkey*, Europe Report No. 225, April 30, 2013.

[146] Mac McClelland, "How to Build a Perfect Refugee Camp," *New York Times Magazine*, February 13, 2014.

[147] See, e.g., ORSAM (Center for Middle Eastern Strategic Studies), *The Situation of Syrian Refugees in the Neighboring Countries: Findings, Conclusions and Recommendations*, Report No: 189, April 2014, pp. 16-17.

---

towns near the Syrian border, with opinion polls reflecting widespread opposition to continued refugee inflows.[148]

In July 2014, the U.N. Security Council adopted Resolution 2165, which permits humanitarian aid for those affected by Syria's civil war to enter Syrian territory from two Turkish border crossings (along with two other crossings – one with Jordan, one with Iraq) irrespective of the Syrian government's approval. Shipments from Turkey have begun.[149]

Iraq

For Turkey, strong governance in Iraq to counter resurgent trends of violence and instability has been important due to Turkish interests in denying the PKK use of Iraqi territory for its safe havens; discouraging the cross-border spread of Kurdish separatist sentiment; countering Iranian influence; and accessing Iraq's potentially lucrative export markets and ample energy resources (which could eventually lessen Turkey's dependence on Iranian and Russian energy imports). Starting in late 2007, U.S. willingness to provide greater counterterrorism support to Turkey in its struggle against the PKK helped move U.S.-Turkey priorities in Iraq toward greater alignment after fallout from the U.S.-led 2003 invasion (discussed above).

Without a U.S. military mission in Iraq, Turkey's influence appears to be more significant. Iraqi Prime Minister Nouri al Maliki, a Shiite, has accused Turkey of undue interference in Iraqi internal affairs. This is likely due to Turkey's increasingly close economic—especially energy—ties to the autonomous Kurdish Regional Government (KRG) in northern Iraq, as well as support that Turkey has provided to Sunni Arab Iraqi leaders.

Observers debate the extent to which Turkish energy dealings with the KRG might enable greater Kurdish autonomy or endanger Iraq's unity. In May 2013, Erdogan announced that a Turkish state-owned company and ExxonMobil would engage in oil exploration with the KRG in northern Iraq.[150] In June, the KRG announced a reportedly Turkey-approved plan to complete a new pipeline that would feed into an existing Iraqi pipeline.[151] Subsequent reports have discussed the possible construction of a second oil pipeline and a natural gas pipeline over the next few years. The Maliki government claims that Turkey-KRG dealings violate Iraq's sovereignty, with disputes ongoing over questions of constitutionality and revenue-sharing.[152] ExxonMobil's and Chevron's reported involvement in northern Iraqi exploration may complicate reported efforts by U.S. officials to discourage Turkey from provoking Maliki, even as his rule and worsening ethnic tensions and sectarian violence raise questions about the viability of Iraq's unity, democracy, and constitution. Turkey renewed high-level political exchanges with the Maliki government in 2013

---

[148] Kemal Kirisci, "Syrian Refugees in Turkey: Bracing for the Long Haul," Brookings Institution, Up Front Blog, February 20, 2014.

[149] Michelle Nichols, "First U.N. aid convoy enters Syria without government consent," *Reuters*, July 24, 2014.

[150] "Turkey's state-run TPAO joins with Exxon, Iraqi Kurds in oil exploration," *Reuters*, May 15, 2013.

[151] Julia King and Peg Mackey, "UPDATE 1-Iraqi Kurds say new oil pipeline to Turkey to start soon," *Reuters*, June 19, 2013.

[152] The Maliki government's concerns appear to be exacerbated by reports that at least one company (the Turkish-British joint venture Genel Energy) is exporting oil from KRG-controlled sources via truck through Turkey, bypassing the Iraqi pipeline completely. Olgu Okumus, "US Complicates Turkey's Energy Interests in Iraq, Iran," *Al-Monitor Turkey Pulse*, May 7, 2013.

---

as part of an apparent effort to reassure the United States and other regional actors that Turkey seeks to promote stability, not undermine it.

The new KRG pipeline began sending oil to Turkey's port of Ceyhan in December 2013. Media reports indicate that a number of tankers left port in search of buyers in June 2014. One shipment was reportedly purchased at the Israeli port of Ashkelon, with the proceeds reportedly deposited in a KRG account in Turkey. However, the other tankers—including one that was anchored off the U.S. Gulf Coast in early August 2014 while facing possible U.S. government seizure if it entered U.S. territorial waters—have encountered difficulties because Iraq's central government has threatened legal action against any buyer.[153] It is unclear whether these transactions are a prelude to KRG attempts to gain independence following Kurdish establishment of control over the city of Kirkuk and two major nearby oil fields in June and July 2014, in the wake of the Islamic State's territorial gains in northwestern Iraq at the expense of the Iraqi army. Another possibility is that KRG leaders are seeking negotiating leverage with Baghdad for a deal resolving oil revenue disputes.

Iran

Turkey seems to be seeking a balance between helping the United States contain Iranian regional influence and maintaining relatively normal political and economic ties with Iran, especially given Turkey's dependence on Iranian energy sources as described below. Differing Iranian and Turkish interests in the region, particularly with regard to Syria and Iraq, have led to increased competition for influence. Turkey and Iran have also competed for the admiration of Arab populations on issues such as championing the Palestinian cause. Nevertheless, Turkey has been supportive of the November 2013 international interim agreement on Iran's nuclear program, perhaps in anticipation that potentially more cordial U.S.-Iran relations will reduce constraints on Turkey from increasing trade with Iran.

Turkey agreed in September 2011 to host a U.S. forward-deployed early warning radar at the Kurecik base near the eastern Turkish city of Malatya as part of NATO's ALTBMD system. Most analysts interpret this system as an attempt to counter potential ballistic missile threats to Europe from Iran.[154] An unnamed senior U.S. Administration official was quoted as calling this agreement "probably the biggest strategic decision between the United States and Turkey in the past 15 or 20 years."[155] Some Iranian officials, after initially expressing displeasure with Turkey's decision, stated that Iran would target the radar in Turkey in the event of a U.S. or Israeli airstrike on Iran. During their visit to Tehran in late March 2012, Erdogan and Davutoglu reportedly said on Iranian television that Turkey could have the radar dismantled within six months if "conditions

---

[153] Reportedly, because Iraq does not have diplomatic relations with Israel, it would have difficulty taking legal action in Israel's jurisdiction. Jackie Northam, "Kurds May Have Oil To Export, But Buyers Are Harder To Find," *NPR*, July 15, 2014. Oil trucked from KRG-controlled areas has reportedly already been shipped and sold to buyers in the United States, Israel, Europe, and Latin America. Julia Payne and Ron Bousso, "EXCLUSIVE-Israel, U.S. import disputed oil from Iraqi Kurdistan," *Reuters*, May 15, 2014. See also Dan Murtaugh and Jack Kaskey, "One Kurdish Tanker Waits Off Texas, Another Heads to U.S.," *Bloomberg*, August 1, 2014.

[154] See footnote 11. The radar was activated in late December 2011. "Part of NATO missile defense system goes live in Turkey," *CNN*, January 16, 2012. It is reportedly operated by U.S. personnel from a command center in Diyarbakir, with a Turkish general and his team stationed in Germany to monitor the command and control mechanisms headquartered there for the entire missile defense system. "Malatya radar system to be commanded from Ramstein," *Hurriyet Daily News*, February 4, 2012.

[155] Thom Shanker, "U.S. Hails Deal with Turkey on Missile Shield," *New York Times*, September 15, 2011.

Turkey had put forward to host the radar are not respected"[156]—a likely reference to Turkish leaders' public insistence that data collected from the radar are not to be shared with Israel.[157]

Following some reports that Iran might be assisting the PKK, Iran and Turkey publicly committed in October 2011 to cooperating against the PKK and the Iranian Kurdish separatist organization Party of Free Life of Kurdistan (PJAK) that also maintains safe havens in northern Iraq. At least one analyst predicts that Iran might increase its influence with Iraq's central government and with Iran-friendly Iraqi Kurdish groups to counter Turkey's growing political and economic leverage in Kurdish-controlled areas of northern Iraq.[158]

According to figures provided on the website of the U.S. Energy Information Administration, Iran provides approximately 44% of Turkey's oil imports and 19% of its natural gas imports. Turkey's announcement that it would reduce Iranian oil imports helped it gain an exemption from the U.S. sanctions that took effect in June 2012. Media and official attention in late 2012 and early 2013 focused on a "gold-for-energy" trading practice between Turkey and Iran that was characterized by many as helping Iran circumvent newly instituted international restrictions on access to the global financial system.[159] However, a new U.S. law took effect in July 2013 specifically sanctioning the provision of precious metals to Iran (Section 1245 of P.L. 112-239, National Defense Authorization Act for Fiscal Year 2013, enacted January 2, 2013).[160] Perhaps as a consequence, reports in early 2013 indicated that Turkey may have been reducing gold-for-energy trades with Iran,[161] turning largely to barter-style arrangements permitting Iran to receive goods as a result of its energy trade with Turkey.[162] Additional U.S. and international concerns about Iran's possible use of Turkish companies or institutions to finance and supply its nuclear program and avoid the impact of sanctions largely focus on Turkey's legal standards[163] and on the reported recent profusion of Iranian-financed firms in Turkey.[164]

In April 2013, 47 Members of Congress sent a letter raising many of the concerns described in the previous paragraph with Secretary of State John Kerry and Secretary of the Treasury Jack Lew, and seeking further information from them.[165] It is unclear whether or how Turkish companies

---

[156] "Erdogan, in Iran, says NATO radar could be dismantled if needed," *Today's Zaman*, March 30, 2012.

[157] According to U.S. officials, despite this Turkish insistence, information collected from the radar is coordinated as necessary with the U.S. missile defense radar deployed in Israel. One senior Administration official has been quoted as saying, "Data from all U.S. missile defense assets worldwide, including not only from radars in Turkey and Israel, but from other sensors as well, is fused to maximize the effectiveness of our missile defenses worldwide; this data can be shared with our allies and partners in this effort." Josh Rogin, "Amid tensions, U.S. and Turkey move forward on missile defense," *thecable.foreignpolicy.com*, September 19, 2011. Some Members of Congress had insisted that sharing information for Israel's potential defense be a condition of the radar's placement in Turkey. The text of a September 19, 2011, letter to President Barack Obama from six Senators on this subject is available at http://kirk.senate.gov/?p=press_release&id=299.

[158] Reva Bhalla, "Letter from Kurdistan," Stratfor Geopolitical Weekly, December 10, 2013.

[159] John Daly, "How Far Will Turkey Go in Supporting Sanctions Against Iran?," *Turkey Analyst*, July 5, 2013.

[160] For more general information on this subject, see CRS Report RS20871, *Iran Sanctions*, by Kenneth Katzman.

[161] Asli Kandemir, "Exclusive: Turkey to Iran gold trade wiped out by new U.S. sanction," *Reuters*, February 15, 2013.

[162] Olgu Okumus, "US Complicates Turkey's Energy Interests in Iraq, Iran," *Al-Monitor Turkey Pulse*, May 7, 2013.

[163] Financial Action Task Force Public Statement, Paris, February 22, 2013; Daniel Dombey, "Turkey's last-minute terror laws: will they be enough?," *blogs.ft.com*, February 8, 2013.

[164] "New Iranian firms in Turkey stir front company worries for Ankara," *todayszaman.com*, February 17, 2013.

[165] The text of the letter is available at http://jeffduncan.house.gov/sites/jeffduncan.house.gov/files/Turkey-Iran%20Letter%20%28April%2011%202013%29.pdf.

---

might change their trading practices with Iran in anticipation of potential sanctions relief following the international interim agreement on Iran's nuclear program that took effect in January 2014.

The Crimea Issue—Russia and Ukraine[166]

Russia's March 2014 unilateral annexation of the Crimean peninsula from the Ukraine (through the instrumentality of a Crimean referendum vote to join Russia) raises a number of concerns for Turkey, including the following:

- Increased uncertainty regarding regional security among fellow Black Sea littoral states to Turkey's north at a time when Turkey's southern border (Syria and Iraq) faces major security and refugee crises.

- Possible "collateral damage" to Turkey's security and economic well-being from great power disputes (United States, Russia, European Union) from which it may be excluded.

- Return of historical concerns about Russian regional dominance and disregard for neighbors' sovereignty, heightened by Turkey's energy dependence on Russia (which provides approximately 58% of Turkey's natural gas imports and 10% of its oil imports[167]—also see "Energy Issues" above).

- Potential challenges in managing non-littoral countries' (including the United States and other NATO allies) naval access to the Black Sea.[168]

- How to address the rights and demands of Crimean Tatars, who make up approximately 12% of Crimea's population; largely favor Ukrainian sovereignty over Crimea; and share historical, ethnic, religious, and linguistic ties with Turks.

Although the medium- and long-term implications of Crimea's annexation and the Ukraine crisis are unclear, these developments could increase Turkey's significance as a political and security actor and as an energy transit corridor. They could also lead Turkey to newly calibrate how its interests might influence the nature and extent of its closeness with a number of actors, including the United States, other NATO allies, the European Union, and/or Russia—possibly influencing Turkey's stances on a number of other issues.[169]

---

[166] For more information, see CRS Report RL33460, *Ukraine: Current Issues and U.S. Policy*, by Steven Woehrel; and CRS Report RL33407, *Russian Political, Economic, and Security Issues and U.S. Interests*, coordinated by Jim Nichol and Steven Woehrel.

[167] From the U.S. Energy Information Administration website.

[168] Turkey permits access to the Black Sea through the Bosphorus and Dardanelles Straits pursuant to the terms of the 1936 Montreux Convention, which can sometimes limit the size and volume of U.S. ships permitted to traverse the straits, as during the 2008 Russia-Georgia conflict. See "US warship crosses Bosphorus towards Black Sea," *Agence France Presse*, March 7, 2014.

[169] See, e.g., Soner Cagaptay and James F. Jeffrey, "Turkey's Muted Reaction to the Crimean Crisis," Washington Institute for Near East Policy, PolicyWatch 2219, March 4, 2014.

Possible U.S. Policy Options and Areas of Concern

Although U.S. and Turkish interests and policies intersect in many respects, Turkey's increased regional influence and moves toward military and economic self-reliance have decreased its dependence on the United States. Still, the appeal of U.S. and Western power, prestige, values, and military technology might currently outstrip that of potential competitors.

Members of Congress, through active inquiry into and possible coordination with Obama Administration positions on Turkey, and their own engagement on Turkey-related issues, can consider how various options might serve U.S. interests. One U.S. analyst wrote in December 2011:

> Despite record levels of communication and travel between top leaders in Ankara and Washington, the societal and institutional connections are still in need of revitalization and strengthening.... [C]oordination and policy on Turkey continues to affect vital interests throughout Washington, which ideally must go beyond the administration to the Hill and society at large even if there is short-term turbulence.[170]

Influencing Regional Change and Promoting Stability

Turkey is likely to play a role on key regional security and political issues. In partnering with Turkey to influence regional developments and promote stability, the following options are available for Members of Congress and Obama Administration officials to adopt or continue:

- Determine how to encourage improvement in Turkey's relations with Israel.

- Determine the proper nature and extent of bilateral and NATO military and intelligence cooperation, including joint use of Turkish bases and territory, as well as information sharing to assist in countering the PKK and in facilitating interdiction of illegal arms shipments from other countries or non-state actors.

- Determine whether and how to encourage Turkish influence in Syria and Iraq, and how to link any such influence to regional political, security, and economic order.

- Determine whether and how to coordinate with Turkey to impose and enforce unilateral, multilateral, or international sanctions that have the potential to effectively weaken or change the behavior of regimes or other actors contravening international laws and norms. Examples include the Iranian regime, the Asad regime, and jihadist opposition groups in Syria.

- Determine whether and how U.S. officials and lawmakers should encourage further liberalization and reform in Turkey's domestic arena, given the influence that domestic developments may have on U.S.-Turkey cooperation and regional security.

---

[170] Joshua W. Walker, "U.S.-Turkish Relations: Modesty and Revitalization," *On Turkey*, German Marshall Fund of the United States, December 15, 2011.

Arms Sales and Military/Security Assistance

Turkey continues to seek advanced U.S. military equipment (i.e., fighter aircraft and helicopters), and its defense industry participates in joint ventures with the United States (e.g., on the F-35 Joint Strike Fighter). However, as exemplified by Turkey's possible deal with Chinese government-owned CPMIEC on air and missile defense (see "China-Turkey Air and Missile Defense Cooperation?" below), Turkey's growing defense industry appears increasingly willing to engage in arms import-export transactions or joint military exercises with non-NATO countries, such as China, Russia, Pakistan, and South Korea. This suggests that Turkey is interested in maximizing its acquisition of technology, diversifying its defense relationships, and decreasing its dependence on the United States. It is unclear how Turkey's procurement relationships with other countries might affect the availability of U.S. arms to Turkey.

Table 3. Significant U.S.-Origin Arms Transfers or Possible Arms Transfers to Turkey

(congressional notifications since 2006)

Amount/Description	FMS or DCS	Year Cong. Notice	Contract	Delivery	Primary Contractor(s)	Estimated Cost
100 F-35A Joint Strike Fighter aircraft	DCS	2006		2017-2025 (expected if contract signed)	Lockheed Martin	$11 billion-$15 billion
30 F-16C Block 50 Fighter aircraft and associated equipment	FMS	2006	2009	2012 (estimated complete)	Consortium (Lockheed Martin, Raytheon, and others)	$1.8 billion
48 AGM-84H SLAM-ER Air-surface missiles	FMS	2006	2006	2012 (24 estimated)	Boeing	$162 million
105 AIM-9X SIDEWINDER Air-air missiles (SRAAM)	FMS	2007		2008 (127 estimated — 2012 notice listed below)	Raytheon	$71 million
51 Block II Tactical HARPOON Anti-ship missiles	FMS	2007	2008 (for at least 4)	2011 (4 estimated	McDonnell Douglas (Boeing)	$159 million
100 MK-54 MAKO Torpedoes	FMS	2007	2009	2011-2013 (75 estimated)	Raytheon	$105 million
30 AAQ-33 SNIPER and AN/AAQ-13 LANTIRN Aircraft electro-optical systems (targeting and navigation pods)	FMS	2008	2009	2012 (30 estimated)	Lockheed Martin	$200 million
6 MK 41 Vertical Launch Systems for Ship-air missiles	FMS	2008	Signed	2011 (3 estimated)	Lockheed Martin	$227 million

Amount/Description	FMS or DCS	Year			Primary Contractor(s)	Estimated Cost
		Cong. Notice	Contract	Delivery		
107 AIM-120C-7 Air-air missiles (AMRAAM)	FMS	2008	Signed	2013 (25 estimated)	Raytheon	$157 million
400 RIM-162 Ship-air missiles (ESSM)	DCS	2009		2011-2013 (142 estimated)	Raytheon	$300 million
72 PATRIOT Advanced Capability Missiles (PAC-3), 197 PATRIOT Guidance Enhanced Missiles, and associated equipment	FMS	2009			Raytheon and Lockheed Martin	$4 billion
14 CH-47F CHINOOK Helicopters	FMS	2009	2011 (for 6)	2014 (expected)	Boeing	$1.2 billion
3 AH-1W SUPER COBRA Attack Helicopters	FMS	2011		2012	N/A (from U.S. Marine Corps inventory)	$111 million
117 AIM-9X-2 SIDEWINDER Block II Air-air missiles (SRAAM) and associated equipment	FMS	2012		(2007 notice listed above)	Raytheon	$140 million
48 MK-48 Mod 6 Advanced Technology All-Up-Round (AUR) Warshot torpedoes and associated equipment	FMS	2014			Raytheon and Lockheed Martin	$170 million

Source: Defense Security Cooperation Agency, Stockholm International Peace Research Institute Arms Transfer Database, *Defense News, Hurriyet Daily News*, Global Security.

Notes: All figures and dates are approximate; blank entries indicate that data is unknown or not applicable. FMS refers to "Foreign Military Sales" contemplated between the U.S. government and Turkey, while DCS refers to "Direct Commercial Sales" contemplated between private U.S. companies and Turkey.

Turkey had reportedly been particularly interested since 2008 in acquiring armed drone aircraft from the United States to use against the PKK.[171] In light of recent reports, it is unclear to what extent Turkey's aspirations to acquire U.S. drones might persist despite possible informal Congressional rejection of Turkey's request in connection with allegations that Turkey disclosed the identities of Israeli intelligence sources to Iran.[172] The Obama Administration redeployed four unarmed U.S. Predator drones from Iraq to Turkey in late 2011 before the end of the U.S. military mission in Iraq—apparently so that the Predators could continue flying surveillance missions in northern Iraq in support of Turkey's efforts to counter the PKK.[173] It is unclear how Turkey's

---

[171] According to *Jane's*, Turkey had sought to purchase four MQ-1 Predator drones and six MQ-9 Reaper drones (more advanced versions of the Predator). "Procurement, Turkey," *Jane's Sentinel Security Assessment - Eastern Mediterranean*, December 16, 2010. Potential sales of Reapers to NATO allies such as the United Kingdom, Germany, Italy, and France have been notified to Congress since 2008.

[172] See footnote 25.

[173] "US deployed Predators to Incirlik: Davutoglu," *Hurriyet Daily News*, November 13, 2011. According to then Secretary of Defense Panetta, the Iraqi government gave the United States permission to keep flying Predator drones on (continued...)

ongoing negotiations with the PKK may affect its plans to procure drones and other military equipment.

U.S. military and security assistance programs for Turkey are designed to cultivate closeness in relationships and practices between Turkish military officers and security officials and their U.S. counterparts. These programs also seek to counter terrorist and criminal networks that are active in the region, including those which historically have operated within and across Turkey's borders.[174] In April 2013, Turkish police stated that in February they had detained conspirators in potential Al Qaeda-linked terrorist plots against the U.S. embassy in Ankara and two other sites.[175]

Table 4. Recent U.S. Foreign Assistance to Turkey

($ in millions)

Account	FY2010	FY2011	FY2012	FY2013	FY2014 Request	FY2015 Request
International Military Education and Training (IMET)	5.0	4.0	4.0	3.4	3.3	3.3
International Narcotics Control and Law Enforcement (INCLE)	—	0.5	0.5	—	—	
Nonproliferation, Antiterrorism, Demining, and Related Programs (NADR)	3.0	1.4	1.1	0.9	0.8	1.5
Total	**8.0**	**5.9**	**5.6**	**4.3**	**4.2**	**4.8**

Source: U.S. Department of State.

Note: All amounts are approximate.

Possible "Armenian Genocide Resolution"

Congress's involvement on Turkey-Armenia issues has the potential to strongly influence U.S.-Turkey relations. On April 10, 2014, the Senate Foreign Relations Committee voted to report S.Res. 410 for consideration by the full Senate. The language of S.Res. 410 characterizes actions of the Ottoman Empire against Armenians during World War I as genocide. It is unclear whether the Senate will vote on the proposed resolution. In 1975 (H.J.Res. 148) and 1984 (H.J.Res. 247), the House passed proposed joint resolutions that referred to "victims of genocide" of Armenian ancestry from 1915 and 1915-1923, respectively.[176] Neither proposed joint resolution came to a

---

(...continued)

surveillance missions over northern Iraq. Craig Whitlock, "U.S. drones allowed in Iraqi skies," *washingtonpost.com/blogs/checkpoint-washington*, December 16, 2011.

[174] State Department FY2014 Congressional Budget Justification, Foreign Operations, Annex: Regional Perspectives, pp. 404-406. The United States and Turkey co-chair the Global Counterterrorism Forum. See Co-Chairs' Fact Sheet: About the Counterterrorism Forum, State Department website, April 2, 2014, at http://www.state.gov/r/pa/prs/ps/2014/04/224313.htm.

[175] Sebnem Arsu, "U.S. Embassy in Turkey Said to Be Targeted," *New York Times*, April 12, 2013.

[176] Unlike H.Res. 252 and some proposed resolutions similar to it, neither H.J.Res. 148 nor H.J.Res. 247 explicitly identified the Ottoman Empire or its authorities as perpetrators of the purported genocide. H.J.Res. 247 stated that "one and one-half million people of Armenian ancestry" were "the victims of the genocide perpetrated in Turkey".

vote in the Senate. A number of other proposed resolutions characterizing these World War I-era events as genocide have been reported by various congressional committees (see **Appendix F** for a list). Moreover, President Ronald Reagan referred to a "genocide of the Armenians" during a Holocaust Remembrance Day speech in 1981.[177]

In response to a March 2010 vote in the House Foreign Affairs Committee to report a proposed resolution on the subject (H.Res. 252) for consideration by the full House, Turkey recalled its ambassador from the United States for one month, and at least one prominent AKP lawmaker reportedly warned that "the relationship would be downgraded on every level" in the event of House passage of the resolution. This warning was commonly interpreted as including a threat to curtail, at least partially or temporarily, U.S. access to Turkish bases and territory for transporting non-lethal cargo to missions in Iraq and Afghanistan.[178]

Although Turkish officials voiced displeasure at the Senate Foreign Relations Committee's action on April 10, on April 23—the eve of the annual remembrance day for the events in question— Prime Minister Erdogan made a speech that included the following statements:

> In Turkey, expressing different opinions and thoughts freely on the events of 1915 is the requirement of a pluralistic perspective as well as of a culture of democracy and modernity....
>
> Nevertheless, using the events of 1915 as an excuse for hostility against Turkey and turning this issue into a matter of political conflict is inadmissible....
>
> It is our hope and belief that the peoples of an ancient and unique geography, who share similar customs and manners will be able to talk to each other about the past with maturity and to remember together their losses in a decent manner. And it is with this hope and belief that we wish that the Armenians who lost their lives in the context of the early twentieth century rest in peace, and we convey our condolences to their grandchildren.[179]

U.S. and EU officials both welcomed the speech as a positive step and expressed hope that it would help lead to additional progress toward Turkish-Armenian reconciliation.[180]

Advocates of recognizing a genocide are to commemorate the event's 100th anniversary in 2015. In addition to past statements or actions by U.S. policymakers (as described above), at least 20 countries other than Armenia have recognized the Ottoman-era deaths as genocide in some way, including 11 of the 28 EU member states.[181]

---

[177] Additionally, in a May 1951 written statement to the International Court of Justice, the Truman Administration cited "Turkish massacres of Armenians" as one of three "outstanding examples of the crime of genocide" (along with Roman persecution of Christians and Nazi extermination of Jews and Poles). International Court of Justice, *Reservations on the Convention of the Prevention and Punishment of the Crime of Genocide: Advisory Opinion of May 28, 1951: Pleadings, Arguments, Documents*, p. 25.

[178] Robert Tait and Ewen McCaskill, "Turkey threatens 'serious consequences' after US vote on Armenian genocide," *Guardian* (UK), March 5, 2010.

[179] Translated text of statement available at http://www.hurriyetdailynews.com/turkish-pm-erdogans-april-23-statement-on-armenian-issue-in-english.aspx?pageID=238&nID=65454&NewsCatID=359.

[180] Arslan, op. cit.

[181] The EU states recognizing a genocide are France, Germany, Italy, Sweden, Belgium, the Netherlands, Lithuania, Poland, Slovakia, Greece, and Cyprus. The European Parliament has also recognized the deaths as genocide.

Bilateral Trade Promotion

Although successive U.S. Administrations have cited the importance of increased trade with Turkey, and the Obama Administration has reemphasized this in articulating its vision for a multifaceted bilateral strategic relationship,[182] it is unclear how effective government efforts to promote U.S.-Turkey trade can be. Bilateral trade has expanded in recent years, although the gap (in favor of the United States) has widened since 2009 both in actual terms and in percentage terms.[183] The U.S. government has designated Turkey as a priority market under the National Export Initiative and the interagency Trade Policy Coordination Committee has developed an Export Enhancement Strategy for Turkey.[184] On its side, the Turkish Ministry of Economy has identified six U.S. states as the focus of its efforts to increase bilateral trade: California, Texas, New York, Florida, Illinois, and Georgia.[185]

Turkish officials have occasionally proposed a U.S.-Turkey free or preferential trade agreement or U.S. legislation establishing qualified industrial zones (QIZs) in Turkey without success.[186] Some policymakers and observers claim that even if past economic conditions may have limited U.S. trade with Turkey, recent growth in Turkish consumer demand, quality of products and services, and global competitiveness and brand recognition have increased Turkey's value as an import source, target market, and place of investment for U.S. companies.[187]

With U.S. and EU officials in the process of negotiating a possible Transatlantic Trade and Investment Partnership (TTIP), some analysts and advocates have called for Turkey to be included in whatever discussions may occur.[188] In October 2013, Turkey's official media agency quoted the chairman of a prominent Turkish business confederation as saying that Speaker of the House John Boehner agreed in private meetings that Turkey's exclusion from a potential TTIP

[182] The two countries signed a Bilateral Investment Treaty in 1990 and a Trade and Investment Framework Agreement in 1999. Annual meetings for the U.S.-Turkey Framework for Strategic Economic and Commercial Cooperation began in 2010 at the cabinet ministerial level.

[183] See, e.g., Sidar Global Advisors, *U.S.-Turkish Economic Relations in a New Era: Analysis and Recommendations for a Stronger Strategic Partnership*, Turkish Industry & Business Association (TUSIAD) and U.S. Chamber of Commerce, March 2012.

[184] For more detailed information on bilateral efforts to promote trade, see White House Fact Sheet: U.S.-Turkey Economic Partnership, May 16, 2013; U.S. Department of Commerce Fact Sheet: U.S.-Turkey Framework for Strategic Economic and Commercial Cooperation, October 14, 2010.

[185] Information provided to CRS by Turkish Ministry of Economy, September 2011.

[186] Turkey's customs union with the EU (see **Appendix E**) apparently would preclude a free trade or preferential agreement between the United States and Turkey absent a similar U.S.-EU agreement. See Turkish Ministry of Economy website at http://www.economy.gov.tr/index.cfm?sayfa=tradeagreements&bolum=fta&region=0. The 2012 Albright-Hadley report encouraged the pursuit of a U.S.-Turkey free or preferential trade agreement or other measures emphasizing "market access, regulatory compatibility, business facilitation, assistance for small and medium-sized enterprises, and promotion of trade in cutting-edge technologies". Council on Foreign Relations, op. cit., pp. 12-13. Additionally, a March 2012 report jointly sponsored by the Turkish Industry & Business Association (TUSIAD) and the U.S. Chamber of Commerce recommended that U.S. and Turkish trade and investment promotion agencies align strategies and use resources efficiently to "achieve certain mutually set benchmarks and goals." See Sidar Global Advisors, op. cit.

[187] See, e.g., Mark Scott, "In Turkey, Western Companies Find Stability and Growth," *New York Times*, December 23, 2011.

[188] See, e.g., Kemal Kirisci, "Don't Forget Free Trade with Turkey," *nationalinterest.org*, April 15, 2013; Bahadir Kaleagasi and Baris Ornarli, Turkish Industry and Business Association (TUSIAD), "Why Turkey belongs to transatlantic economy," *thehill.com/blogs*, March 12, 2013.

would be unfair.[189] Because of its customs union with the EU, analysts conclude that Turkey would—absent an agreement with the United States or EU to the contrary—be required to comply with all the trade obligations of a potential TTIP without gaining any of the direct benefits.[190] Some analysts estimate possible consequences to Turkey to include a 2.5% (roughly $20 billion) long-term loss in national income, and the loss of close to 95,000 jobs.[191] Although a parallel trade deal with Turkey would therefore not be necessary for the United States to gain preferential access to Turkey's market, proponents of a U.S.-Turkey trade agreement argue that it would be important in reinforcing overall bilateral relations and in anchoring Turkey's ties with the West.[192] It is unclear to what extent the technical complexity of a U.S.-EU trade negotiation may raise difficulties for Turkey's participation in the process.

During Prime Minister Erdogan's May 2013 visit to Washington, DC, Vice President Joe Biden was quoted as saying at a U.S. Chamber of Commerce meeting that Erdogan and President Obama "had agreed to begin efforts for a Free Trade Agreement."[193] However, one analyst has written that because of potential obstacles, including probable stances "by the Armenian and Greek lobbies against a free trade agreement with Turkey, one cannot be too sanguine about the chances of passage in Congress of a free trade agreement with Turkey, even with the President's influence."[194]

Conclusion

Turkey's importance to the United States may have increased relative to previous eras of U.S.-Turkey cooperation because of Turkey's geopolitical importance, growing economy, and greater foreign policy assertiveness. Congressional action on arms sales, a potential free trade agreement, or a possible "Armenian genocide resolution" could have implications for the bilateral alliance, particularly if Members of Congress link their stances on these issues to U.S.-Turkey tensions or disagreements over Israel, other Middle East-related issues, or Chinese-Turkish defense industrial cooperation.

---

[189] *Anadolu Agency*, quoted in "US House speaker tells TÜSİAD that Turkey should not be excluded from transatlantic trade alliance," *Hurriyet Daily News*, October 12, 2013.

[190] Turkish officials are now publicly raising the possibility of renegotiating the customs union because of this lack of mutuality.

[191] Two German reports cited in Kirisci, *Turkey and the Transatlantic Trade and Investment Partnership: Boosting the Model Partnership with the United States*, op. cit., footnote 29.

[192] Kirisci, *Turkey and the Transatlantic Trade and Investment Partnership: Boosting the Model Partnership with the United States*, op. cit. See also Tyson Barker and Cenk Sidar, "U.S.-EU Trade Talks Risk Damaging Turkey Ties," *Bloomberg View*, May 12, 2013.

[193] "Biden: US and Turkey to work for FTA," *worldbulletin.net*, May 17, 2013. Biden was also quoted as saying, "We will not only keep Turkey informed of every step of the negotiation with the EU, but we believe that if in fact, we can get by some of the divisions and the differences we have with regard to free trade agreements, that if we can get there before the time we settle the EU new trade agreement, that it will be a great opportunity for Turkey." Ibid. Officially, the two countries decided in May 2013 to "establish a bilateral High Level Committee led by the Ministry of Economy of Turkey and the Office of the U.S. Trade Representative, associated with the Framework for Strategic Economic and Commercial Cooperation, with the ultimate objective of continuing to deepen our economic relations and liberalize trade." White House Fact Sheet: U.S.-Turkey Economic Partnership, May 16, 2013.

[194] Mark Meirowitz, "A Realistic and Candid Look at Turkish-U.S. Relations," Magazine of American-Turkish Council: 32nd Annual Conference on U.S.-Turkish Relations, June 2-5, 2013.

The positions that Members of Congress take on specific issues concerning Turkey—including defense cooperation, trade promotion, and Turkish domestic developments—will shape perceptions of U.S. priorities at a critical time for global and regional stability and for the Turkish republic's political and constitutional evolution. This could influence Turkish leaders' future foreign policy rhetoric, decisions, and alignments, which in turn will likely have implications for regional security and for Turkey's EU accession prospects. Congressional positions could also have some influence on Turkey's commitment to civilian-led, democratic government that enshrines individual, media, and minority rights; rule of law; and due process.

Appendix A. Profiles of Key Figures in Turkey

Prime Minister Recep Tayyip Erdogan

Prime Minister Erdogan (pronounced *air-doe-wan*) was born in Istanbul in 1954 and spent much of his childhood in his family's ancestral hometown of Rize on the Black Sea coast. He and his family returned to Istanbul for his teenage years, and he attended a religious *imam hatip* school. In the 1970s, Erdogan studied business at what is today Marmara University, played soccer semi-professionally, and became politically active with the National Salvation Party, led by the pioneering Turkish Islamist figure (and eventual prime minister) Necmettin Erbakan. After the military banned all political parties in the wake of its 1980 coup, Erdogan became a business consultant and executive. When political life in Turkey resumed, Erdogan became a prominent local leader and organizer for Erbakan's new Welfare Party.

Erdogan was elected mayor of Istanbul in 1994 at the beginning of a wave of Islamist political victories in Turkey in the mid-1990s. He was removed from office, imprisoned for six months, and banned from parliamentary politics for religious incitement after he recited a poem in the southeastern city of Siirt in December 1997 that included the passage (translated from Turkish): "The mosques are our barracks, the domes our helmets, the minarets our bayonets and the faithful our soldiers."

After Erbakan's government resigned under military pressure in 1997 and the Welfare Party was disbanded, Erdogan became the founding chairman of the AKP in 2001. The AKP won a decisive electoral victory in 2002, securing the single-party rule that it has maintained since. After the election, a legal change allowed Erdogan to run for parliament in a 2003 special election in Siirt, and after he won, Erdogan replaced Abdullah Gul as prime minister.

Erdogan and his personal popularity and charisma have been at the center of much of the domestic and foreign policy change that has occurred in Turkey in the past decade. His criticism of Israel and its actions has by some accounts boosted his popularity at home and throughout the Muslim Middle East. Subsequently, Erdogan's stances on unrest and transition in countries such as Egypt, Libya, and Syria also attracted significant regional and global attention.

Erdogan's rhetoric and actions have come under even greater scrutiny since June 2013. Some reports describe Erdogan as less amenable to political compromise in part due to his long tenure in office, and as relying increasingly on a small group of trusted advisors, including intelligence chief Hakan Fidan.[195] Recent leaks of audio recordings supposedly reflecting discussions Erdogan had with his son Bilal about transferring large sums of money to avoid detection has fueled media speculation about the tenability of Erdogan's power and position, particularly in light of coming elections and Erdogan's candidacy for the presidency. There have been recent signs of distancing between Erdogan and President Obama in light of various events complicating bilateral relations, after several years of reports that Erdogan and Obama have enjoyed positive personal interaction.[196]

---

[195] Adam Entous and Joe Parkinson, "Turkey's Spymaster Plots Own Course on Syria," *Wall Street Journal*, October 10, 2013.

[196] Peterson, op. cit. The Abramowitz-Edelman Report states that Erdogan places a high regard on U.S. praise. Bipartisan Policy Center, op. cit., p. 10.

Erdogan is married and has two sons and two daughters. His wife Emine and daughters wear the headscarf. He is not fluent in English but his understanding may be improving. Observers have speculated about his health, particularly following a November 2011 surgical procedure to remove stomach polyps. He has said that he does not have cancer.

President Abdullah Gul

President Gul was born in 1950 in Kayseri in central Turkey. He studied economics in Turkey and England, and received his Ph.D. from Istanbul University, becoming a university professor and an economist at the Islamic Development Bank in Jeddah, Saudi Arabia. Gul was first elected to parliament from Kayseri in 1991 as a member of the Islamist Welfare Party and served as a minister in and spokesman for the coalition government it briefly headed in 1996-1997. After the Welfare Party was disbanded, Gul stayed on in parliament as a reform-minded member of the Islamist Virtue Party. Gul served on parliamentary assemblies of NATO and the Council of Europe. When the AKP was formed in 2001, he became deputy chairman and—briefly—its first prime minister after the successful election of 2002. When Erdogan took over the prime ministry in 2003, Gul became Turkey's foreign minister and helped accelerate Turkey's EU accession process.

In 2007, the AKP nominated Gul for the presidency amid substantial secularist opposition, partly owing to statements from his early political career that indicated distaste for the secular nature of Turkey's republic. Parliament nevertheless elected Gul president. Many observers believe him to be a moderating influence on the Erdogan government, as reflected in his approach to various issues since the June 2013 nationwide protests—though some have expressed skepticism over whether Gul is able or willing to meaningfully check Erdogan's power. Gul is not running for a second presidential term, presumably in deference to Erdogan, and has stated that he would not desire to succeed Erdogan as prime minister. Nevertheless, speculation continues regarding Gul's possible succession of Erdogan, perhaps at least as a caretaker until the 2015 presidential elections,[197] as well as Gul's long-term plans in the domestic or international arena.

Gul is married with two sons and a daughter. His wife Hayrunissa and daughter wear the headscarf. He speaks fluent English.

Foreign Minister Ahmet Davutoglu

Foreign Minister Davutoglu was born in 1959 in Konya in central Turkey. He attended a German international school in Istanbul and received a Ph.D. in Political Science and International Relations from Bosphorus University. He became a university professor, spending time in Malaysia in the early 1990s before establishing himself as a scholar known for applying academic theory to practical matters of Turkish foreign policy and national security strategy. His book *Strategic Depth*, which was published in 2001 and has been translated into other languages but not English, is thought by some to represent a blueprint of sorts for the policies Davutoglu has since helped implement.

---

[197] See, e.g., Semih Idiz, "Gul's next move depends on Erdogan," *Al-Monitor Turkey Pulse*, June 3, 2014; Gulten Ustuntag, "Parliament seeks formula to choose next prime minister," *todayszaman.com*, July 12, 2014.

Following the AKP's victory in 2002, Davutoglu was appointed chief foreign policy advisor to the prime minister. Upon his appointment as foreign minister in 2009, he quickly gained renown for articulating and applying the concepts of strategic depth and "zero problems with neighbors." He advocates for a preeminent role for Turkey in its surrounding region, but disputes the characterization of his policies by some observers as "neo-Ottomanism." Davutoglu's policies have encountered domestic and international criticism given the challenges Turkey has recently faced from regional problems in countries such as Syria, Iraq, and Egypt (as discussed above). He won an AKP parliamentary seat for the first time in June 2011.

Davutoglu is married with four children. His wife Sare is a medical doctor. He speaks fluent English, as well as German and Arabic.

Opposition Leader Kemal Kilicdaroglu

Kilicdaroglu, the leader of the main opposition CHP, was born in 1948 in Tunceli province in eastern Turkey. After receiving an economics degree from what is now Gazi University in Ankara, Kilicdaroglu had a civil service career—first with the Finance Ministry, then as the director-general of the Social Security Organization. After retiring from the civil service, Kilicdaroglu became politically active with the CHP and was elected to parliament from Istanbul in 2002. He gained national prominence for his efforts to root out corruption among AKP officials and the AKP-affiliated mayor of Ankara. When CHP leader Deniz Baykal was forced to resign over a videotape sex scandal in May 2010, Kilicdaroglu was elected to replace him. He made his first official visit to the United States in December 2013.

Kilicdaroglu is married with a son and two daughters. He is an Alevi and speaks fluent French.

PKK Leader Abdullah Ocalan

Abdullah Ocalan was born in or around 1949 in southeastern Turkey (near Sanliurfa). After attending vocational high school in Ankara, Ocalan served in civil service posts in Diyarbakir and Istanbul until enrolling at Ankara University in 1971. As his interest developed in socialism and Kurdish nationalism, Ocalan was jailed for seven months in 1972 for participating in an illegal student demonstration. His time in prison with other activists helped inspire his political ambitions, and he became increasingly politically active upon his release. Ocalan founded the Marxist-Leninist-influenced PKK in 1978 and launched a separatist militant campaign against Turkish security forces—while also attacking the traditional Kurdish chieftain class—in 1984. He used Syrian territory as a safe haven. Syria forced Ocalan to leave in 1998 after Turkey threatened war for harboring him. After traveling to several different countries, Ocalan was captured in February 1999 in Kenya—possibly with U.S. help—and was turned over to Turkish authorities. The PKK declared a cease-fire shortly thereafter. Ocalan was sentenced to death, in a trial later ruled unfair by the European Court of Human Rights, but when Turkey abolished the death penalty in 2002, the sentence was commuted to life imprisonment. He resides in a maximum-security prison on the island of Imrali in the Sea of Marmara, and was in solitary confinement until 2009.

Although acting PKK leader Murat Karayilan and other commanders have exercised direct control over PKK operations during Ocalan's imprisonment, some observers believe that Ocalan still ultimately controls the PKK through proxies. PKK violence resumed in 2003 and has since continued off-and-on until the most recent cease-fire that Ocalan and Karayilan called in March

2013. Ocalan has indicated that the organization is seeking a negotiated resolution that does not require forming a Kurdish state, and is engaging in talks with Turkish officials to that end.

Appendix B. List of Selected Turkish-Related Organizations in the United States

American Friends of Turkey (http://afot.us/)

American Research Institute in Turkey (http://ccat.sas.upenn.edu/ARIT/)

American Turkish Society (http://www.americanturkishsociety.org/)

American-Turkish Council (http://www.the-atc.org/)

Assembly of Turkish American Associations (http://www.ataa.org/)—component associations in 18 states and the District of Columbia

Ataturk Society of America (http://www.ataturksociety.org/)

Federation of Turkish American Associations

Institute of Turkish Studies (http://turkishstudies.org/)

SETA Foundation for Political, Economic and Social Research (http://setadc.org)

Turkic American Alliance (http://www.turkicamericanalliance.org/)

- West America Turkic Council (West region)—includes Pacifica Institute
- Turkish American Federation of Midwest (Midwest region)—includes Niagara Foundation
- Turquoise Council of Americans and Eurasians (South region)—includes Institute of Interfaith Dialog
- Turkic American Federation of Southeast (Southeast region)—includes Istanbul Center
- Council of Turkic American Associations (Northeast region)—includes Turkish Cultural Center
- Mid Atlantic Federation of Turkic American Associations (Mid-Atlantic region)—includes Rumi Forum
- Rethink Institute (housed at Turkic American Alliance headquarters in Washington, DC)

Turkish Coalition of America (http://www.tc-america.org/)

Turkish Confederation of Businessmen and Industrialists (TUSKON) (http://www.tuskonus.org/tuskon.php)

Turkish Cultural Foundation (http://www.turkishculturalfoundation.org/)

Turkish Industry & Business Association (TUSIAD) (http://www.tusiad.org/)

Turkish Policy Center (http://www.turkishpolicycenter.org/)

Union of Chambers and Commodity Exchanges of Turkey (TOBB) (http://www.tobb.org.tr/)

Appendix C. Historical Context

Changes to the old Kemalist order did not materialize suddenly with the AKP's rise to power. They reflect long-standing dynamics in Turkish politics and society that continue to evolve within Turkey's existing constitutional framework. Popular desires to allow greater public space for traditional Islamic-oriented lifestyles manifested themselves politically as early as the 1950s during the rule of Turkey's first democratically elected leader, Adnan Menderes. Menderes was eventually overthrown by a military-led coup in 1960 (and subsequently hanged), and the military continued to discourage the overt influence of religion in politics, intervening again in 1971 and 1980 to replace governments that it deemed had lost control of the country or had steered it away from secularism or toward ideological extremes.

The military allowed Deputy Prime Minister for Economic Affairs (later Prime Minister and President) Turgut Ozal to begin liberalizing the traditionally statist Turkish economy following its restoration of internal order in 1980. This helped set in motion a chain of events leading to the economic and political empowerment of millions of Turks hailing from traditional communities removed from Turkey's more secular urban centers. Subsequent social and political developments reflected accommodation of this rising middle class—many of whom migrated to bigger cities— and their values. For example, *imam hatip* religious schools, initially established for young males seeking clerical careers, became widely attended by youth from religiously conservative families. In 1997, the military compelled Turkey's first-ever Islamist-led coalition government to resign, but junior members of the coalition-leading Refah (Welfare) Party went on to form the AKP,[198] which they characterize as a center-right reformist party without an Islamist agenda.

---

[198] AKP members generally use the acronym "AK Party" or "AK," partly because the Turkish word *ak* means "clean" and "unblemished," thus presenting an image of incorruptibility.

Appendix D. Religious Minorities in Turkey

While U.S. constitutional law prohibits the excessive entanglement of the government with religion, republican Turkey has maintained secularism or "laicism" by controlling or closely overseeing religious activities in the country. This is partly to prevent religion from influencing state actors and institutions, as it did during previous centuries of Ottoman rule. Sunni Muslims, although not monolithic in their views on freedom of worship, have better recourse than other religious adherents to the democratic process for accommodation of their views because of their majority status. Minority Muslim sects (most prominently, the Alevis) and non-Muslim religions largely depend on legal appeals, political advocacy, and support from Western countries to protect their rights in Turkey.

Christians and Jews

U.S. concerns focus largely on the rights of established Christian and Jewish communities and religious leaderships and their associated foundations and organizations within Turkey to choose leaders, train clergy, own property, and otherwise function independently of the Turkish government.[199] Some Members of Congress routinely express grievances through proposed congressional resolutions and through letters to the President and to Turkish leaders on behalf of the Ecumenical (Greek Orthodox) Patriarchate of Constantinople, the spiritual center of Orthodox Christianity based in Istanbul.[200] On December 13, 2011, for example, the House passed H.Res. 306—"Urging the Republic of Turkey to safeguard its Christian heritage and to return confiscated church properties"—by voice vote.[201] Also, as mentioned above, in late June, the House Foreign Affairs Committee reported the Turkey Christian Churches Accountability Act (H.R. 4347).[202]

In an April 2012 interview with the *Chicago Tribune*, Ecumenical Patriarch Bartholomew was quoted as saying that recent changes in Turkey

---

[199] The U.S. Commission on International Religious Freedom (USCIRF) included Turkey on its watch list from 2009 to 2011, and, in a decision disputed among the commissioners, recommended in 2012 that the State Department list Turkey as a "country of particular concern" (CPC). In USCIRF's 2013 report, Turkey was not included on either the watch list (now reclassified as "Tier 2") or the CPC list, but on a separate list of countries being "monitored." Four of the eight commissioners dissented, saying that Turkey's 2012 CPC listing was a mistake, but that it should remain on the watch list/Tier 2. Turkey was included in Tier 2 for the 2014 report, with one commissioner dissenting. For additional information on Turkey's religious minorities, see the State Department's International Religious Freedom Report for 2013.

[200] The Patriarchate traces its roots to the Apostle Andrew. The most commonly articulated congressional grievances on behalf of the Patriarchate—whose ecumenicity is not acknowledged by the Turkish government, but also not objected to when acknowledged by others—are the non-operation of the Halki Theological School on Heybeliada Island near Istanbul, the requirement that the Patriarch be a Turkish citizen, and the failure of the Turkish government to return previously confiscated properties.

[201] H.Res. 306 was sponsored by Representative Edward Royce, now Chairman of the House Foreign Affairs Committee. An identically worded proposed resolution was introduced in the Senate in March 2012 as S.Res. 392. Proposed resolutions from the 113th Congress include H.Res. 136 ("Urging Turkey to respect the rights and religious freedoms of the Ecumenical Patriarchate"), and H.Res. 188 ("Calling upon the Government of Turkey to facilitate the reopening of the Ecumenical Patriarchate's Theological School of Halki without condition or further delay."). H.Res. 188 was forwarded to the House Foreign Affairs Committee on November 19, 2013, by its Subcommittee on Europe, Eurasia, and Emerging Threats.

[202] See footnote 18.

have been extremely positive. Years ago, you couldn't have dreamed of the changes. You couldn't have believed it. The prime minister has promised to restore properties confiscated from Christians and Jews years ago. He has promised to reopen the Orthodox seminary at Halki, which has been closed for many years. Of course, we have concerns in some areas, and there are legal questions remaining, but the Orthodox-Islamic dialogue has been extremely positive. More positive than I ever would have imagined.[203]

Patriarch Bartholomew, along with various U.S. and European officials, continues to press for the reopening of the Halki Theological School. In March 2013, Erdogan reportedly conditioned Halki's reopening on measures by Greece to accommodate its Muslim community.[204] Meanwhile, according to late 2013 media reports, Turkey is in the process of converting at least two historic Christian churches into mosques, and may be considering additional conversions.[205] The U.S. Commission on International Religious Freedom (USCIRF) released a statement in May 2014 calling a bill introduced in Turkey's parliament to convert Istanbul's Hagia Sophia into a mosque "misguided."[206] An advisor to Prime Minister Erdogan was cited shortly thereafter as indicating that there were no plans to alter Hagia Sophia's status, despite some popular calls to do so.[207]

At various times in the Turkish Republic's history, the state has confiscated the properties of religious groups as part of its efforts to control religious life in the country. In late August 2011, Erdogan announced that Turkey would return properties confiscated since the adoption of a 1935 law governing religious foundations, to the extent the properties are still held publicly.[208] Many of these properties were confiscated following a Turkish High Court of Appeals ruling in 1974 that had invalidated religious foundations' abilities to acquire real estate.[209] Properties subject to return include schools, orphanages, cemeteries, commercial properties, and hospitals affiliated with various Christian churches and Turkey's Jewish community. According to one report, "The government's willingness to explore restitution does not yet cover the hundreds, if not thousands, of property seizures from individuals, or the takeovers that occurred before 1936. An even more contentious point is confiscation that occurred prior to the formation of the Republic of Turkey in 1923."[210] Prior to Erdogan's 2011 decree, which followed an earlier 2008 amendment to the law on religious foundations, the European Court of Human Rights made multiple rulings requiring Turkey to pay compensation to various religious-affiliated organizations after earlier attempts by the government to remedy the situation did not satisfy the organizations. According to the USCIRF's 2013 annual report:

---

[203] John Kass, "With faith and hope, Turkey builds a new identity," *Chicago Tribune*, April 11, 2012. Some sources indicate that Prime Minister Erdogan promised at a March 2012 meeting with President Obama in Seoul, South Korea, that he would reopen the Halki seminary. See, e.g., David Ignatius, "Obama's friend in Turkey," *Washington Post*, June 7, 2012.

[204] "PM indicates opening Halki Seminary depends on reciprocal gesture by Greece," *todayszaman.com*, March 30, 2013.

[205] Peter Kenyon, "Some Turkish Churches Get Makeovers—As Mosques," *NPR*, December 3, 2013; Dorian Jones, "Turkish Leaders Aim to Turn Hagia Sophia Back into a Mosque," *Voice of America*, November 29, 2013.

[206] USCIRF website, "Turkey: Statement on Hagia Sophia," May 21, 2014.

[207] Ayla Jean Yackley, "Muslims pray to turn Turkey's greatest monument back into a mosque," *Reuters*, May 30, 2014.

[208] According to reports, the foundations would receive compensation for property since transferred to third parties. See Sebnum Arsu, "Turkish Government to Return Seized Property to Religious Minorities," *New York Times*, August 29, 2011.

[209] The ability for these foundations to acquire real estate has since been restored. The 1974 court ruling came at a time of high Turkish-Greek tensions with the outbreak of conflict in Cyprus.

[210] Dorian Jones, "Turkey: Making Room for Religious Minorities," *EurasiaNet.org*, October 3, 2011.

Between the passage of the 2008 amendment and August 2011, approximately 200 properties were reportedly returned to religious minority foundations of various denominations.

Additionally, according to the USCIRF's 2014 annual report:

Since 2011, 340 properties – valued, according to the government, at more than 2.5 billion Turkish Lira – have been returned or compensated for.[211] However, 1,000 applications were denied, 800 for lack of information and 200 for other reasons. Some communities allege bias, consider the process very slow, and claim that compensation has been insufficient.

Alevis

Most Muslims in Turkey are Sunni, but 10 million to 20 million are Alevis (of whom about 20% are ethnic Kurds). The Alevi community has some relation to Shiism[212] and may contain strands from pre-Islamic Anatolian and Christian traditions.[213] Alevism has been traditionally influenced by Sufi mysticism that emphasizes believers' individual spiritual paths, but it defies precise description owing to its lack of centralized leadership and reliance on oral traditions historically kept secret from outsiders. According to the State Department's International Religious Freedom Report for 2012, "The government considers Alevism a heterodox Muslim sect and does not financially support religious worship for Alevi Muslims." Alevis have long been among the strongest supporters of Turkey's secular state, which they reportedly perceive as their protector from the Sunni majority.[214] Recent developments appear to have heightened Sunni-Alevi tensions, including those pertaining to the June 2013 protests, the Syrian conflict and Turkey's policy (Arab Alawites in Syria and southern Turkey are a distinct Shia-related religious community, but are often likened to Alevis by the region's Sunni Muslims), and frustrated expectations among some Alevi leaders that the government reform package announced in September 2013 would address their grievances.[215]

---

[211] For example, in January 2013, 190 hectares of forestland surrounding the Halki Theological School were returned to the Greek Orthodox foundation listed as its owner-of-record. Fatma Disli Zibak, "Turkey makes largest property return to Greek Orthodox community," *todayszaman.com*, January 11, 2013.

[212] For information comparing and contrasting Sunnism and Shiism, see CRS Report RS21745, *Islam: Sunnis and Shiites*, by Christopher M. Blanchard.

[213] For additional historical background, see Elise Massicard, *The Alevis in Turkey and Europe: Identity and managing territorial diversity*, New York: Routledge, 2013, pp. 11-18.

[214] According to a Boston University anthropologist who studies modern Turkish society, "Alevis suffered centuries of oppression under the Ottomans, who accused them of not being truly Muslim and suspected them of colluding with the Shi'i Persians against the empire. Alevi Kurds were victims of the early republic's Turkification policies and were massacred by the thousands in Dersim [now called Tunceli] in 1937-39. In the 1970s, Alevis became associated with socialist and other leftist movements, while the political right was dominated by Sunni Muslims. An explosive mix of sectarian cleavages, class polarization, and political violence led to communal massacres of Alevis in five major cities in 1977 and 1978, setting the stage for the 1980 coup." Jenny White, *Muslim Nationalism and the New Turks*, Princeton: Princeton University Press, 2013, p. 14. See also Bipartisan Policy Center, op. cit., footnote 62.

[215] Bipartisan Policy Center, op. cit., p. 28.

Appendix E. Additional Foreign Policy Issues

European Union[216]

The Turkish government uses its demographic profile to support its bid for EU membership, arguing that the country would bring a young, dynamic population to the aging ranks of Europe and boost EU influence in the Muslim world. Turkey first sought to associate itself with what was then the European Economic Community (EEC) in 1959, and Turkey and the EEC entered into an agreement of association in 1963. Since the end of 1995, Turkey has had a full customs union with the EU, which is viewed by many observers as one of the primary drivers of the competitive surge of Turkey's economy during the 2000s.[217] Turkey also is a member of the Council of Europe, along with several other non-EU states (including Russia), and is subject to the jurisdiction of the Council's European Court of Human Rights.

EU accession talks, which began in 2005, have been stalled owing to the opposition of key EU states—most notably France and Germany—to Turkey's full membership. Opponents generally give empirical reasons for their positions, but many analysts argue that resistance to Turkish EU accession is rooted in a fear that Turkey's large Muslim population would fundamentally change the cultural character of the EU and dilute the power of the EU's founding Western European states to drive the policy agenda. As mentioned above, Turkey's unwillingness to normalize diplomatic and trade relations with EU member Cyprus presents a major obstacle to its accession prospects.[218] Other EU concerns over Turkey's qualifications for membership center on the treatment of Kurds and religious minorities, media freedoms, women's rights, and the proper and transparent functioning of Turkey's democratic and legal systems.[219] One U.S.-based European analyst writes, "Turkey's process of alignment with EU laws and standards is still very incomplete and interest in this goal seems to have weakened as political forces that once embraced the goal [as a means for facilitating Turkish domestic reform] have become stronger and more self-reliant."[220] Debate regarding Turkey's alignment with EU standards has intensified as a result of the June 2013 protests[221] and (as discussed above) recent domestic controversies and laws on the judiciary and the Internet, though accession talks opened on a new chapter of the *acquis communautaire* in November 2013.

Turkish domestic expectations of and support for full accession to the EU were apparently already waning before the June 2013 protests and post-December 17, 2013, controversies, and

---

[216] For more information on this subject, see archived CRS Report RS22517, *European Union Enlargement: A Status Report on Turkey's Accession Negotiations*, by Vincent L. Morelli; and CRS Report RS21344, *European Union Enlargement*, by Kristin Archick and Vincent L. Morelli.

[217] Council on Foreign Relations, op. cit., p. 18.

[218] Turkey's unwillingness to open its ports to Greek Cypriot trade according to the Additional Protocol that it signed at the outset of the accession process in 2005 prompted the EU Council to block eight out of the 35 chapters of the *acquis communautaire* that Turkey would be required to meet to the Council's satisfaction in order to gain EU membership. France blocked five additional chapters in 2007 and the Republic of Cyprus blocked six in 2009. France unblocked one chapter in early 2013, in what some analysts interpreted as a portent for better prospects of Turkey's eventual accession. Thus far, one of the chapters has been fully negotiated, and 14 others have been opened.

[219] European Commission Staff Working Document, *Turkey 2013 Progress Report*, October 16, 2013.

[220] Emiliano Alessandri, "Turkey-EU Relations: Back to Basics?," *On Turkey*, German Marshall Fund of the United States, February 27, 2013.

[221] European Parliament Resolution of 13 June 2013 on the Situation in Turkey (2013/2664(RSP)).

before fundamental concerns arose over the economic and political soundness of the EU as a result of the eurozone crisis.[222] In September 2013, Turkey's then Minister for EU Affairs and chief accession negotiator, Egeman Bagis, was quoted as saying, "In the long run I think Turkey will end up like Norway. We will be at European standards, very closely aligned but not as a member."[223] Nevertheless, the EU provides over $1 billion in annual pre-accession financial and technical assistance to Turkey aimed at harmonizing its economy, society, bureaucracy, and political system with those of EU members.[224]

Cyprus and the Eastern Mediterranean[225]

Since Cyprus became independent of the United Kingdom in 1960, Turkey has viewed itself and has acted as the protector of the island's ethnic Turkish minority from potential mistreatment by the ethnic Greek majority.[226] Responding to Greek and Cypriot political developments that raised concerns about a possible Greek annexation of Cyprus, Turkey's military intervened in 1974[227] and established control over the northern third of the island, prompting an almost total ethnic and de facto political division along geographical lines. That division persists today and is the subject of continuing international efforts aimed at reunification.[228] Additionally, according to a *New York Times* article, "after the 1974 invasion, an estimated 150,000 Turkish settlers arrived in the north of Cyprus, many of them poor and agrarian Turks from the mainland, who Greek Cypriots say are illegal immigrants used by Turkey as a demographic weapon."[229] The ethnic Greek-ruled Republic of Cyprus is internationally recognized as having jurisdiction over the entire island, while the de facto Turkish Republic of Northern Cyprus in the northern third has only Turkish recognition. Congress imposed an embargo on military grants and arms sales to Turkey from

---

[222] Dan Bilefsky, "For Turkey, Lure of Tie to Europe Is Fading," *New York Times*, December 4, 2011. According to the *Transatlantic Trends* surveys of the German Marshall Fund of the United States, the percentage of Turks who think that Turkish EU membership would be a good thing was 73% in 2004 and 44% in 2013.

[223] Alex Spillius, "Turkey 'will probably never be EU member,'" *telegraph.co.uk*, September 21, 2013.

[224] See http://ec.europa.eu/enlargement/instruments/funding-by-country/turkey/index_en htm for further information.

[225] For more information on this subject, see CRS Report R41136, *Cyprus: Reunification Proving Elusive*, by Vincent L. Morelli.

[226] Turkey views its protective role as justified given its status as one of the three guaranteeing powers of the 1960 Treaty of Guarantee that was signed at the time Cyprus gained its independence. The United Kingdom and Greece are the other two guarantors.

[227] Turkish intervention in Cyprus with U.S.-supplied arms prompted Congress to impose an embargo on military assistance and arms sales to Turkey from 1975 to 1978. This Cold War-era disruption in U.S.-Turkey relations is often cited by analysts as a major factor in Turkey's continuing efforts to avoid overdependence on the United States or any other country for military equipment or expertise.

[228] Turkey retains between 30,000 and 40,000 troops on the island (supplemented by approximately 5,000 Turkish Cypriot soldiers and 26,000 reserves). "Turkish Republic of Northern Cyprus," *Jane's Sentinel Security Assessment - Eastern Mediterranean*, October 30, 2009. This is countered by a Greek Cypriot force of approximately 12,000 (including roughly 1,300 Greek officers and soldiers seconded to Cyprus) with reported access to 50,000 reserves. "Cyprus," *Jane's World Armies*, November 3, 2011. The United Nations maintains a peacekeeping mission (UNFICYP) of approximately 900 personnel within a buffer zone headquartered in Cyprus's divided capital of Nicosia (known as Lefkosa in Turkish). Since the mission's inception in 1964, UNFICYP has suffered 179 fatalities. The United Kingdom maintains approximately 3,000 personnel at two sovereign military bases on the southern portion of the island at Akrotiri and Dhekelia.

[229] Dan Bilefsky, "On Cyprus Beach, Stubborn Relic of Conflict," *New York Times*, August 3, 2012. As of July 2014, the CIA World Factbook estimates Cyprus's total population to be 1,172,458 (77% Greek, 18% Turkish, 5% other).

1975 to 1978 in response to Turkey's use of U.S.-supplied weapons in the 1974 conflict, and several Members remain interested in Cyprus-related issues.[230]

The Republic of Cyprus's accession to the EU in 2004 and Turkey's refusal to normalize political and commercial relations with it are seen as a major obstacle to Turkey's EU membership aspirations. The Cyprus dilemma also hinders effective EU-NATO defense cooperation. Moreover, EU accession may have reduced incentives for Cyprus's Greek population to make concessions toward a reunification deal. The Greek Cypriots rejected by referendum a United Nations reunification plan (called the Annan plan after then Secretary-General Kofi Annan) in 2004 that the Turkish Cypriot population accepted. Turkey and Turkish Cypriot leaders claim that the Turkish Cypriot regime's lack of international recognition unfairly denies its people basic economic and political rights, particularly through barriers to trade with and travel to countries other than Turkey.

Turkey and Turkish Cypriots have assertively opposed efforts by the Republic of Cyprus and other Eastern Mediterranean countries—most notably Israel—to agree upon a division of offshore energy drilling rights without a solution to the question of the island's unification.[231] The Republic of Cyprus appears to anticipate considerable future export revenue from drilling in the Aphrodite gas field off Cyprus's southern coast. In the wake of the Republic of Cyprus's early 2013 euro bailout, and given analyses indicating that the most efficient way for the Republic to export its newfound energy resources would be by constructing a pipeline to Turkey, some observers speculate that the potential financial benefits of unification justify renewed diplomatic efforts to that end.[232] In testimony at a July 11, 2013, Senate Foreign Relations Committee hearing considering her nomination as Assistant Secretary of State for European and Eurasian Affairs, Victoria Nuland (who was subsequently confirmed in September 2013) said:

> I think circumstances are changing, attitudes are changing, not just within Cyprus but also in Greece and in Turkey, and we have to capitalize on that. We also have natural gas off the coast of Turkey, which is off the coast of Cyprus, which is a powerful motivator for getting to the solution that we all want which is a bizonal bicommunal federation that can share the benefits.

Greek and Turkish Cypriots formally resumed negotiations in February 2014, and Vice President Biden visited Cyprus in May 2014 and offered U.S. assistance as part of his encouragement for a settlement.[233]

---

[230] See, e.g., from the 112th Congress, H.Res. 676 (To expose and halt the Republic of Turkey's illegal colonization of the Republic of Cyprus with non-Cypriot populations, to support Cyprus in its efforts to control all of its territory, to end Turkey's illegal occupation of northern Cyprus, and to exploit its energy resources without illegal interference by Turkey.); S.Con.Res. 47 (A concurrent resolution expressing the sense of Congress on the sovereignty of the Republic of Cyprus over all of the territory of the island of Cypress [sic].); and H.R. 2597 (American-Owned Property in Occupied Cyprus Claims Act).

[231] "Gas drilling heightens east Mediterranean tension," *UPI*, September 16, 2011.

[232] See, e.g., "Divided they fall," *Economist*, April 27, 2013. Additionally, Greek Cypriots elected Nicos Anastasiades as president of the Republic of Cyprus in February 2013. Anastasiades is one of the few Greek Cypriot leaders to have backed the 2004 Annan Plan for reunification.

[233] White House website, Remarks by Vice President Joe Biden at an Official Lunch with President Nicos Anastasiades of Cyprus, Nicosia, Cyprus, May 22, 2014.

Armenia[234]

In late 2009, Turkey and Armenia, aided by Swiss mediation, agreed to joint protocols that would have normalized relations and opened borders between the two countries. They also would have called for a dialogue and impartial examination of the historical record with respect to "existing problems," widely believed to refer to the issue of World War I-era deaths of hundreds of thousands of Armenians through the actions of Ottoman Empire authorities. Turkish leaders were unwilling to push for parliamentary ratification of the protocols, however, due to Azerbaijani objections to Turkey-Armenia normalization prior to desired progress on the issue of Nagorno-Karabakh.[235] Azerbaijan influences Turkish policy on this issue because of its close cultural and economic ties with Turkey, particularly as Azerbaijan is a key energy supplier. Another possible cause for Turkish reluctance was a 2010 Armenian constitutional court ruling that indicated inflexibility on the genocide issue. Subsequently, Turkey and Armenia have made little or no progress toward ratifying the protocols or otherwise normalizing their relations, though the protocols remain under consideration in Turkey's parliament.[236] The tenor of relations between Turkey and Armenia could be an important factor in a potential congressional debate over a future genocide resolution.

Other International Relationships

As Turkey continues to exercise increased political and economic influence, it seeks to establish and strengthen relationships with non-Western global powers. As discussed above, it is expanding trade and defense industrial ties with China and Russia. It is doing the same with other countries in Asia and Africa.

Turkey additionally seeks to expand the scope of its geographical influence, with its officials sometimes comparing its historical links and influence with certain countries—especially former territories of the Ottoman Empire—to the relationship of Britain with its commonwealth. Through hands-on political involvement, as well as increased private trade and investment and public humanitarian and development projects, Turkey has enhanced its influence and image as a leading Muslim-majority democracy with Muslim-populated countries not only in the greater Middle East, but also in the Balkans, the Caucasus and Central Asia, and sub-Saharan Africa.[237]

---

[234] For more information, see CRS Report RL33453, *Armenia, Azerbaijan, and Georgia: Political Developments and Implications for U.S. Interests*, by Jim Nichol and Steven Woehrel.

[235] Nagorno-Karabakh is a predominantly ethnic-Armenian-populated enclave within Azerbaijan's international borders. Disputes over its status led to armed conflict in 1991 in parallel with the Soviet Union's dissolution and the independence of both Armenia and Azerbaijan. The conflict ended with a 1994 ceasefire, but Armenian troops still occupy portions of the territory. The Minsk Group of the Organization for Security and Cooperation in Europe (co-chaired by the United States, Russia, and France, and including both Armenia and Azerbaijan, as well as Turkey and a number of other European countries) has been trying to negotiate a permanent settlement since then.

[236] In the meantime, Turkey and Azerbaijan signed a 10-year security and mutual assistance agreement in August 2010.

[237] See, e.g., Hajrudin Somun, "Turkish Foreign Policy in the Balkans and 'Neo-Ottomanism': A Personal Account," *Insight Turkey*, vol. 13, no. 3, summer 2011; Yigal Schleifer, "Turkey's Neo-Ottoman Problem," *World Politics Review*, February 16, 2010; Greg Bruno, "Turkey's Near Abroad," Council on Foreign Relations Analysis Brief, September 19, 2008.

Appendix F. Congressional Committee Reports of Armenian Genocide-Related Proposed Resolutions

Date Reported or of Vote for Report	Proposed Resolution(s)	Committee
April 5, 1984	S.J.Res. 87	Senate Judiciary
September 28, 1984	S.Res. 241	Senate Foreign Relations
July 9, 1985	H.J.Res. 192	House Post Office and Civil Service
July 23, 1987	H.J.Res. 132	House Post Office and Civil Service
August 3, 1987	H.Res. 238	House Rules
October 18, 1989	S.J.Res. 212	Senate Judiciary
October 11, 2000	H.Res. 596 and H.Res. 625	House Rules
May 22, 2003	H.Res. 193	House Judiciary
September 15, 2005	H.Res. 316 and H.Con.Res. 195	House International Relations
March 29, 2007	S.Res. 65	Senate Foreign Relations
October 10, 2007	H.Res. 106	House Foreign Affairs
March 4, 2010	H.Res. 252	House Foreign Affairs
April 10, 2014	S.Res. 410	Senate Foreign Relations

Author Contact Information

Jim Zanotti
Specialist in Middle Eastern Affairs
jzanotti@crs.loc.gov, 7-1441